About the Author

Vaul Impera is the originator and creator of Immortalaeism, and the first to adopt it as a philosophical/spiritual paradigm. He has been offered international law to fight against sex trades by Parliament of Canada. He has been offered leadership positions in the army, and he has been offered high positions in the Church.

Vaul Impera

IMMORTALAEISM II

AUSTIN MACAULEY PUBLISHERS™
LONDON • CAMBRIDGE • NEW YORK • SHARJAH

A CIP catalogue record for this title is available from the British Library.

ISBN 9781787104174 (Paperback)
ISBN 9781787104181 (Hardback)
ISBN 9781398417618 (ePub e-book)

www.austinmacauley.com

First Published 2021
Austin Macauley Publishers Ltd®
1 Canada Square
Canary Wharf
London
E14 5AA

Table of Contents

POWER II

And Now, The Essence of My Power.
-Vaul Impera

1.   Prime Cause

1.1 First Cause

A prime cause will draw from the sources of power in the cosmos/universe for its matrix. Accessing a power comes by creating a pool for the spirit of that power, from the truth of the cosmos, in his life. That is, by walking in the way of *that* power, he learns to generate its spirit and the affinity of it from which he may live by either creating it or drawing it from the unmanifested (spiritus primus), which is the spirits that he uses for his life and power, and he fills himself with these spirits at different times and locations in his life. He must understand how to create the talisman of his power, and there it will collect and pool, it is an eternal pool of spirit unending where he may draw the spirit of his power, that is, the spirit of power. To know the spirits of the cosmos that are in the world is what I call being behind the world, in the ethereal realm, apostolically, where the world is a spiritual labyrinth of creative powers, gates, symbols, impassible divisions, passes, secrets and domains that are not trespassed. He must find his way *behind* the world which is to, 'TOXYCANT' – the creative realm of power and spirit that is before the physical world, which is the unmanifested realm. Toxycant is the name I (Vaul) bestow upon this realm in Immortalaeism. It is the realm from where all of the spirits of the world are pooling and interacting, with gates and symbols and paths to other spirits that can and cannot be accessed because of what has been accomplished in the spirit of him. From these spirits are all of the ideologies in their representations. This eternal realm is from where all of the ends of the human possibility are represented, and the paths of one's life and circumstance are mapped by its connecting structure. The golden spirit is the base spirit, that can be made into any spirit, and by the worlds decree, the spirits are being made after the will. Many balances fall into reality by the equating that are in Toxycant (Libra).

Power is connected to us at all times, and it cannot be deceived or disconnected except by death. Power holds the truth of power itself in equality, so that power will always distribute what is equal for a propensity. Power understands what must take place before a cause and after a cause, so that the necessary factors of the chains of events that support a cause and that follow a cause are implemented due to the dispensations of power itself. Power also dispenses according to identity and the way of power itself. First Causes that require power are sometimes difficult to imagine, because they are creative. In order to force a cause, such as an experiment, or a factory requires the knowledge of sources, and understanding that power will bring the same result again. Power will gather to a prime cause, and it will surround the cause with its manifestation of power, and it will knit the event into the fate of the world, and in powers light, it will bring forth the true event. The manipulation of the cosmos and power's acceptance of this testifies to creative genius.

Prime cause means that the first has been instated. It imparts origination. It is the original, and the true form an entity, so that from originality it bears its origin and original invention, where is begins a new cause in the great schemata. It cannot be denied or expressed with such a second image or defect that would render the first ineffective. In metaphysics, it is the original elements that comprise a thing in itself. Without replication, and without being able to be denied, it is first before all, and unable to be moved. It has a unique position in the universe, where it is rendered the original of all that may be like it, and its true form will never change. The prime cause also sets in motion that which follows, in a chain of cause and effect, after itself. There are many prime causes, and many original ideas. We must possess the prime cause if we are to fully understand a thing in itself. For other regard, there is initiation that may be made by originating and developing one's own field of knowledge and invention. That is power to oneself, it is a development, and what may be found may be surreal and different from what is normalized, and possessing it will produce different effects in the person, but with Processionalism it may be found what those effects may be, and whether or not they are beneficial. If two men of equal power compete for the head of authority, selection will be granted to the one who has greater knowledge, because of what may be produced for the realm. Power always selects that which is most beneficial for its causes. Power will never deny what 'is', in that entities and events and all involved, speak for what they are. Strength and knowledge are two aspects of the same mode, and all things/advantages must pool into power in order to create a power. The power that created will continue to channel to that which was created, and the imposter will find a supporting power that desires the reward of the creation. A pure cosmology.

1.2 Possessors

Possessors are first as governors. Because they possess, they are the first to understand, and thus, they are instated as the owners of such and such property or dominion. Those that possess are in the unique position of being that which receives for that which they possess, and they are the overwatch of the dominion. In specific and different fields of knowledge, that which is under the authority of an individual will benefit him, and it will pertain to a certain field of knowledge which is his special benefit. For example, in the case of fertility, such as a fertility goddess, the knowledge which she would govern benefits her, and she is the possessor of such an affinity and dominion, so that the possession of an affinity means inclusion into the category of being one that possesses the right and the knowledge to govern a dominion after that affinity. As prime cause, it is their lives which circumnavigate and initiate all of the extent of that said dominion, and no other. Thus, it is their power, and theirs alone. As such, they should receive the full merit and stature for their position, as is in accordance with virtue, lest we be not fair. In addition, there are those that seek to replicate, those that do not own the origination of the work, and many are these men, who seek the reputation and the rewards of the true owners and heirs. The reputation of justice is desired, for example, and many gods and angels are demons, and have great detail about justice, and in the end, they are manipulative and evil, the gains of justice are spent by promulgating further recklessness. Immediately, in Immortalaeism, we shall say of those who are of a false reputation (a different power), that they do not exist to us, and their works are not counted at all, and neither are their words, obviously, because they challenge the realm. They are a group of imposters, and once discovered as such, they are useful as mercenaries, or less. They have taken the way of murder, and they are bloody nations, and bloody false gods, with false reputations for approval, to stand with them and appear as having stature, so that they may receive a morsel to eat. To have Prime Cause must literally mean that there is nothing else influencing, but instead, a cause originating from within. (The problem with United Cause is that it belongs to you as long as you can keep it, as it is based on a communal understanding. Prime Cause may always be kept, it is sure, and it is sound, and it is privileged because one will not be moved by another, due to universal pivoted means, where all things must come to the gates, and may not venture to the side in any way, so that by having prime cause, I methodically sort through the world in its relation to me, by watching what my Cause determines for me, and not by forcing or attempting a determination.)

To say that there is a connexion between prime cause and causes of power, is to iterate that there is a witness between events in the world, and events in the 'heavens'. To say this is to mean that individual acts of will are understood by powers, and that powers will regard each act differently. Is it different than praying to a god, to understand universal power and its manifestations? How should a power, or power itself, understand that my cause is more worthy than an imposter of myself? Cosmology is the anthropomorphism of the cosmos, in which powers substantiate gods, but in order for a power to respond to a god and act with his will, it must benefit individually, understanding how a response from a god solicits its power, and thus, powers must be solicited properly, according to cosmology. In order to solicit from a power, he must have the same intelligence in order to use the power, which is equal. Thus, power manifests in the vacuum of what is equal to his composition and understanding. To be identical with some-thing is to mean that he may acquire as many of those things as is within his propensity. It is given to him, because he can manifest the power of that thing. In this conjuring, he is powerful because he has invented a prime cause, that is, he has realized how to access a power individually, without any previous knowledge of that cause. To draw the power is a primal cause, he must access the power first, and the imposter must access it secondarily, and in this event, different types of power will be distributed, because he draws power with the truth of his will and being, and power gives him the manifestation of his being, because power cannot provide except that which is equal. Power is taken from a source of power, and the permission of power grants that he may obtain a certain amount, and it is from this that he lives and understands, so that his understanding is taught by power itself. Do we say that power does not distribute with equality for action and propensity? No, power usually teaches what is equal for what is equal, which is an inherent universal truth. But power also teaches what a thing is in respect of other things, so that the value of a power is innumerably greater than what can be provided by other powers. A disjunctive rebellion (rejection) of an idea is contrary, but an opposite does not present itself, and it would not depend upon existing ideas or the rejection itself for its reality. They have an unsatisfactory condition which is only a denial, while the real contender of power must have an independent *power* in-itself. The law-tables and the evidences of the realms and their demonstrations are worthless. The power to create and the power to destroy, a cosmic interchange. The power of the hierarchy of the world is that each person possesses the same capabilities, but how does he find his way, so that the matters of the greatest threats and problems do not challenge him until he knows no greater power in the world than the alignments of times and powers. The survival of a civilization. The Immortalae have their place as guards.

1.3 Statements

Those that state in originality are given the power of that dominion, which for whatever has been referenced. Another statement may be made by someone that was not a part of the origination, but it must be an original statement, or else it is only a duplicate. How good is the duplicate? It is fabrica falsus spiritus, that is, it is made from a false power, so it matters not. The sound of the truth of the matter is heard by truth itself, and also by the universe, as it validates such false knowledge as false, as stated in my original work 'Power'. This is true as the words reach the Prime Cause itself in the metaphysics, and the reverberant sound is not the same as the original, so the sound is false to the duplicated statement. In this, the originator of an individual idea has expressed the truth of the Prime Cause, and thus it sounds perfected to those around him. He also has found that knowledge for his people, and the true idea of what they speak of they have validated in the perfection of their thought, and how it reaches that Prime Cause, and they witness that it is true that what they have learned is actual and that it is the truth. Those that practice the theft and destruction of ideas must duplicate, and usually attempt to remove the original, this is an attempt at belonging in the position of the original, and power reads their mongering as false. It views their anti-works to the original, and to the original power as unacceptable, and in this, their power is fated to a terminal end, and the occupation of holding false notions as weighted back to them in disfavor. Their power is evil, and this is why they count works, and duplicate them in other societies, that they may inherit the reward for the work, after the rewards of the evil.

1.4 The Truth Prime Laws of Immortalae

These lists are predeterminations of occurrences.

A: Basic Function (Identity)
1. Innocence
2. War
3. Truth
4. Virtue
5. Godliness
6. Contra
7. Supremacy
8. Elitism
9. Rule
10. Power

B: Immortal Progress (exaltation)
1. Immutable
2. Sourceless
3. Perfect
4. Truth
5. Determination/Predetermination
6. Calculating
7. Council
8. Procession
9. Exaltation
10. Completion

2. Virtue

2.1 Training in Virtue

Virtue is a part of obtaining of the grail of Exiter and the grail of Finality, and in Immortalaeism, virtue is obtained by immortality, power, heroism and martial arts. As innocence is contemplated in value, I understand that virtue equals that which is advantageous in relation to understanding and progress, so that he by proper training, will achieve the virtues that he needs for his life and the trials that he must face.

2.2 Perfected Virtue

In order to find a proper expression of rule, I will demonstrate my effectiveness by providing examples of how virtue compliments a dominion. In this demonstration, I will use individual virtues to express how at the perfection of these said virtues, that dominance is provided in the excellence of the epithets. So, perfected knowledge and wisdom is the knowledge that rules the world. Perfected courage and fearlessness rules men, and rules the world, and is valuable in all things, including war and warriorism (martial arts). Perfected modesty becomes holding people in derision and contempt and exposing false economy, and it is also strength of appearance and regulation of economy, and it is anti-thetical to the concourse of shame. The absolute value of temperance is absolute pro-hibition of certain behaviors, which are then expelled and cleaved from the human appetite, causing a superior intellect and being. Thus, I esteem that in the absolute value of all virtues, that the excellence that I would provoke to myself would consist in me becoming a higher being. Virtue is a part of the knowledge that shapes what is best in life, and the absolute value of virtue, when virtue has finished its work, I command for all those that participate in Immortalae. The Deciphering Key: Vice: libido, mendacium, fur, sicarius, invidia, ira, superbia, gula, odium. (lie, theif, murder, jealousy, anger, pride, gluttony, hate). Virtue: Veritas, iustus, modestia, pacem, integritas, dignitas, fortis, fides, purus (truth, justice, modesty, peace, integrity, dignity, strength, trust, purity).

Between the two orders of being, is the deciphering key between virtue and vice, that properly understands both orbs of power and their power over men, and thus also, what happens between the powers'. This narrow decipher is the truth of what transpires between Good and Evil. The Immortalae shall exercise themselves in all things profitable, and in virtue, and they shall be as gods, and elite warriors knowing the full difference between the Good and the Evil'. As Immortalae, the spiritual realm and its explanations are open forever, and forever before them. The key to deciphering good and evil is in understanding perfected virtue.

2.3 Selecting Virtues

The sphere of dominion of virtue is the excellence of being, to the perfection of being, and all virtues are compiled systematically, and the science of virtue is known to Immortalae. The science of virtue corresponds to the orb of power (which is Toxycant which is the anter-pools of the realm of the understanding of the world by its founding spirits and orders) of virtue, where in the exercise of virtue, all virtues lead to all other virtues, and in the ultimate, virtue increases the capability of character. The virtues of Immortalaeism are power, immortality, heroism and martial arts. There are no other virtues. We must exercise virtue to perfect ourselves, and fight as Guardians in the world. We understand that the apostolic work of perfecting the firmament of our spiritual lives and that of perfecting virtue is that we will enter Toxycant, and we will find our sources of power.

2.4 Code of Morality

As stated in 'Immortalae', only the exemplary will progress to the understandings of Eternal life and Immortality, hence, virtue. I have deduced a method of such advancement, for Processionalism and Immortalae. It is pertinent to me that all virtue is advancement of character. With that being stated, I have pronounced that virtue is the method and is my code of ethics and morality. I find that virtue properly contains power, and purports excellence, it is convenient to immortality and martial arts. As such, I have instated it under the pronouncement of Processionalism, which is advancement.

2.5 Virtue and Power

The power of virtue will come when the individual decides to ascend in virtue, and change their behavior. I care not for the nonsense of the world. In my following book will reiterate proper conduct and power that should be demonstrated in someone that would like to partake in Immortalaeism, to be the epitome of that which we understand is the farthest and the most excellent of qualities. This is not a vain pursuit, it is the attempt of immortality, and that of being a constant in the world, in the heavens, and in the universe, and it is also to prove the excellence of that which one may attain, which has been said in other words as an attempt at all that one may be, at all times, for the greatest cause. The reason why virtue and power are sided together is proficiency of knowledge, which is: the greater the virtue, the greater the power, and knowledge. As I wrote in 'Power', once a method of travel or an architectonic has been succinctly navigated, faster travel is then augmented. In the dominion of knowledge, once virtue and its knowledge are understood sufficiently, then one may graduate to a higher form of knowledge, relevant to those specific virtues. Virtue is the navigation of the soul, and in becoming what destiny would have of the individual, virtue is the exercise by which they become something excellent, or anything at all.

2.6 Constancy

Perfected virtue is perfect character and leads to the perfected spirit that no longer has spiritual death through action. Perfected virtue is required for immortality, it brings universality and singularity. Perfected virtue moves the individual on to a higher set of virtues, which lead to remarkable personality and unique selection of will, combined with personality bringing desirable maturity. What is this process that governs us in life? Where does it lead? What is virtue in creation and in the metaphysics?

Virtue that is progressive must be constant. In this, virtue arrives at its perfection eventually through constancy. Because it is maintained, it is fidelity, so that it may be relied upon. In this, it is trusted, and remarks in a similar fashion to a deity. In this, in creation, we see the mark of constancy in all things natural and elemental, including the heavens. It is the constancy of the cosmos which affirms the creation of virtue, in that man must prove his intelligence by proving constancy. It is in man's being and from no other place that he may attain virtue. Virtue is permanency, and builds the spirit into greater complexity. The way of power is virtue, because greater ability, and personal character, and is arrived at through fidelity to a virtue, or a cause, where a cause, such as justice, becomes the shape of personal intelligence. We, as Immortalae, must retain knowledge through virtue in order to access processional leaps of intelligence, and manifested growth of being. This brings us superior definition of spiritual and intellectual intelligence. Virtue then, becomes the method of shaping character and growth, based in individual identity, because virtue accommodates understanding. Every time virtue is acted upon, from infancy, it means 'I understand', in being. Virtue then is the nourishment of intelligence which causes him to grow. Virtue affirms idealism, in that virtue is drawn from the permanency of virtues place in the metaphysics, as infinite, and they are knit into the spirit and intelligence. After time, it becomes the shape of our intelligence, as a mythological creature is the shape and logic of an intelligence represented in a picture of form in spirit. The ability of power is expressed through virtue, and virtue is the perfection of completed action, thus, to not achieve virtue is deficient, which exposes error.

Perfected virtue, in essence in the metaphysics, contains everlasting life, and power without death is power forever. In this regard, justice does not matter, and neither does society – what matters is eternal life, and I am teaching that this in part is achieved through perfected virtue, because he will not die spiritually from what he may face any longer because his person is beyond temptation. Virtue is the universal way of saying 'I understand', and virtue is a dispensation and a reward of power, so that one may become more powerful. When greater power is achieved, he must accommodate the power with understanding, which means greater fidelity, which means virtue, which means constancy. Virtue, by sign of intelligence and difference of intelligence to him, points in the end to his spiritual house, and virtue is the way that guides to a final arrival as an Eternal, because he follows his way of intelligence by virtue to the end of a final household. Virtue is the guide to his power, and also to his house of final destination by his intelligence in the heavens. Virtue is the guide to Eternal life, because it restores spiritual life if it is accomplished, and also restores spiritual life if spiritual life is lost through error. In the metaphysics, virtue is bread that leads to eternal life because it affirms spiritual growth, and rewards with the bread daily because it is the virtues of work that bring the fruit of the earth. Immortality is confirmed in virtue because virtue can take spiritual poverty and convert it to wealth. He must not transgress virtue and intelligence and this may be done by use of the spirit of tranquility and peacefulness.

2.7 Pillar of Virtue

The pillars of virtue are erected in the spirit in the metaphysics of man, where eternal, perfect virtue inhabits the pillar, where virtue comes from, in the order that men take virtue. The warrior takes strength first, the cleric takes wisdom. In that the pillars in their organization within the man, are the construct in the metaphysics, he produces a spirit that is as powerful as the pillars, in that they contain the power of everlasting life in the metaphysic. Perfected virtue implies the constancy and permanence of his spirit.

2.8 Aim of Religion

He is not enticed by religion itself. Religion has a way of expressing virtues which are produced from the way of that religion. In Immortalaeism, he may fight the demonic, if he needs to, and he may explore the realms of meditation. The spirit is open to him to experience and to learn. The virtues of Immortalaeism are power, masculinity (or femininity), eternity, immortality, and heroism, and martial art/martial combat. It is the accomplishment of virtue that predicates heaven in many religious codes, because virtue is the result of successfulness in the religion. In Immortalaeism, the code is immortality (and power and martial arts). I understand the dangers of heroism and martial arts, and I understand that courage, in the sense of danger, and bravery, and having these virtues in exercise is necessary for the Immortalae. There are many ways of being a hero, and all of the Immortalae must possess exemplary virtue that sets them at the height of the world in character and demonstration. He must contain the potential within his spirit to lead in the demonstrations of fighting.
Virtue is the method of power, and it is they of expressing mastery of character and universal consistency, that borders an infinite place of distinct power in the cosmos.

2.9 Immortal Energy

'He must have an energy, that speaks of his immortality'. Immortal energy will take the form of a permanent characteristic that cannot be changed, which is the power of his spirit because of who he is. The Earth has many spirits, but in the mastery of virtue his maturity will come into his being and he will find that he is very strong, and deeply united to the cosmos in power. He may attempt the knowledge of knowing how to use universal powers, and how to wield them with his intellect and his spiritual being. The Earth and the Heavens are a part of his Spiritualism. He must find the spirit of fighting.

3. Error

3.1 Destruction

What is error to power? First, it is cessation of power, and it is also futility, so that to error is the decline in power. If the Sun was erroneous, it would interrupt its purpose. Error may also mean deficiency. Of what value is the power of a wall to keep people out if it is deficient? The wall will have lost its power due to mutability, because the power of the wall is broken because it will no longer support its' function. Error is also reasonable, in such that when we locate the source of error and make corrections, we resume power, in our understanding. For this reason we may say that we innately understand power, and we use the consequences of power in order to make actions in the world. However, it is power itself which is what I am speaking of, and not a stone, or a series of stones in a wall. In the view of reasonableness, we may see that great error may mean destruction, or destructiveness. When something is no longer recognizable or repairable, we say that it has been destroyed. The futility of not being able to repair something means that it has no longer any possibility of power, and that it cannot perform its function any longer, for which it was as a function of power. You may purchase a wall with a hole in it and repair it, but if the wall is destroyed, then it no longer has any power to provide a function with.

3.2 Universality and Error

As said in 'Power', the power of a thing is in its ability, power itself understands the fabric of the universe from which it creates a universal draw, an event of cause and effect, so that the enactment of power is the same in every place. We seek to understand what makes the universal aspect of power accessible, so that we understand how source enactments create powerful displays and manifestations that are understandable, which we may replicate, duplicate, manipulate and depend upon that they will happen each time for us, because of universal cause and effect. It is this notion of the universal fabric of the cosmos that brings us cause and effect, and allows us to understand what is behind and what is involved with the distributions of power of the universe. We desire that we would understand how the universe creates itself, and how we are a part of its design. It is because of error and the play of the universe with power that he understands that he is a part of universal design. Immortalaeism views the manifestation of his being as an allusion that he has a great role in the cosmos. Power is also a force, or forces, but it is concerned with the necessary architectonics, which are based in prime cause, which use the perfected originations in order to perform all of the possible constructions and contexts that are in the world. We may see then why it requires greater understanding in order to use higher principles, and achieve things like higher technology. We must finish the equations of THREE before we may understand how to ascend to the equations of FOUR.

3.3 Futility and Human Endeavour

When the truth of a thing accords with its purpose, we may say that it is functioning, and demonstrating its power, and by definition of linguistics, the verification of the power of a thing, accords with what is spoken of it. We may say that error is malfunction, in the effect that it will cause the purpose of a thing to cease, and it will bring unreasonableness into the function of a thing, so that the truth and reasonableness of a thing is corrupted, and it will stop the thing from exhibiting its power in a perfect state. So the perfection of a construct is in its ability to never see error. For this measure in human behavior we have virtue, in human physiology we have health instead of disease, and in human ability we have power instead of futility. So what is the nature of error to us, if in every case of human endeavor and purpose, it brings us dichotomies which mean destruction to us? As discussed in 'POWER', dichotomies are metaphysical properties that have a higher unifying concept. Here I shall say that the power of human endeavor is the higher unifying concept, and the dichotomies are error and destruction of human endeavor, opposed by the perfect function of human endeavor. Can we say that error will take the power of perfect human endeavor from us, but it does also this reasonably, and in a balance of life that we may properly understand, and hold within just scales, hence, Processionalism, I think that would be failure. Instead, the power of our dominion in life must destroy error and deficiency, that is, we must become more powerful, and we must strengthen our dominion, in the eradication of errors and evils. We can certainly say then that power to human endeavor means ability to humans, and that it also means that their function is perfected, and that it is free from error. We may thus view that futility is opposed to ability in respect of power and human endeavor. I shall say that error and dysfunction is also death to us as humans, and that it is loss of power which results in human death. I shall say that moral error is often held as responsible for human death, and I shall say that stupidity, which is typified by error, is also normally responsible for death, and I shall say that the first results in evil and loss of power, while the latter results in powerlessness as well. So I see then that there is a constituent of error in the world, and it brings us decay, destruction, death and change, and that the ultimate effect of error is degeneracy, loss of power. We may see then that the power of change will raise something up, and it will also take it down, over a period of time, and this indicates what is known as the temporal.

3.4 Error and Mutability

Thus I shall say that in the power of a thing is its purpose and function, and in its perfected state it is not subject to destruction, or decay or death, or error, and thus, it will not change, so that it will not die, and thus, it is beyond the power of change, and it is no longer temporal, it is eternal or immortal. I shall also then say, that the most perfected things are everlasting, and they are the products of infinite power. Also, they are the things with the least amount of error. In the ethereal realm, all things are perfected and are everlasting. I will then conclude by saying that by becoming more powerful at destroying that which seeks our destruction, that we may increase in power and destroy change, so that there is no longer a time and a season for all things. This paradox of which I speak, where there is perfection contrasted with imperfection, are the dichotomies and dualisms of which I have previously spoken of in 'Power'. These dualisms are the orbs of life. From which orb shall I take my power from, from the orb or anarchy, or the orb of construction? From the orb of the infinite, or the orb of the finite? An orb is an entire branch of knowledge, taken as knowledge, and the fruit of power that bears a type of power itself. Of all the orbs of power, we must decide from which orbs we do not use, and from which orbs we do obtain power, and which orbs we use indefinitely. I have said that we must take from virtue and not vice, so, life and not death. We must take from power and not futility. These are the metaphysical orbs that exist that comprise what is available in the world in power. It is the notion of change that requires time, it is that which does not change which is eternal. Here we see both orbs of power of the earth flourishing and diminishing, prospering and failing. We must learn as Immortalae, how to properly select from the orbs of the cosmos of duality, but we must accept first that death and error must be deferred in place of Immortality and constancy.

3.5 Error Opposes Perfection (Part I)

I shall then say that error and destruction are opposed to ability and perfection in the duality of the power of a thing, and I shall say that this is a true principle in our world, and that it is proven in buildings, as well as in long life, that the most perfected artifacts have the greatest duration and that they are the most powerful, and perfected things remain. I will say further that perfected things are what make up the realm of the concepts, where I imagine the perfection of all things, and that with perfection is the never-ending, and that it is from the notion of perfected things that we understand a thing in empiricism, because we intend that most things should last in time due to their perfection.

I shall thus say that in the realm of the concepts, in relation to time, that time itself indicates the power of error, and that all things in time will then change, due to error. I shall say that the world is subject to both perfection and imperfection, for in the realm of the concepts, all that is in relation to time will have a duration, but all that is beyond time will have an eternal and an immortal affinity, and will not perish. The realm of concepts is where everything relates conceptually, in its real and actual logic, which is understood reasonably by empirical thought and experience, the concepts are the systematic orders of powers by reason, which is the fairness that is between all essence. The pools and their unification is the location where these powers, by logic and order, pool in Toxycant.

3.5 Error Opposes Perfection (Part II)

The pyramids have been standing for over two-thousand years, are they not more perfect than other buildings? In geometry, it is the complexity and also perfection to perfect shapes that bring strength to a structure, and also the adaption of its form to landforms and the expanse of the world and its forces. We shall say that this qualifies for advanced instead of dysfunctional, and I shall say that advanced means empirically sound, by the concept of conceptual perfection. By the principle of what is advanced, I shall say that adaption to the most powerful, which means the most advanced things in the world, are the most suitable, and those that have no respect for perfection will have no need of excellent things.

3.6 Moral Error

Those who practice religion, but are foolish not to practice goodness, fail and become evil, and with a lack of excellence they prove that they understand nothing of the world, and even of their own life and place in the world. Those that have chosen this error are rejected in regard to Processionalism, and they have chosen the delusion of sufficiency, against progress, and cupidity, and they have appetitive satisfaction of luxury. I will also decree that those that are Processionalists will be advanced, and they will understand and ascribe to excellence and perfection, knowing that nearing perfection in life is the same as drawing close to the Eternal and Immortal, which will lead them closer to the Grail of Exiter, and eternal life and eternal thought, rather than temporal. I shall call the mind that has accomplished eternal thought to be sound mind that understands how to choose things eternally in the world in accordance with the Grail of Exiter.

Moral error I shall also decree as dysfunctional. Civilization typifies the behavior in accordance with their current religious belief that they are reprobate against the established order and economy. I shall say that moral error involves the cessation of life, and demonstrates a lack of understanding, that it is against progress, and it is a disposition of life to accept evils because one is somehow prohibited from success. I shall also say that primitive evil is generally dependent societally upon the good, and without the order and establishment of good society, regression, anarchy and death ensue. I view that evils may depend upon good societies, but that many evil men would perish without society, and it is an error of the deficient in life to depend upon society that is good and depend upon living from it in an evil origin. For example, to live from stealing assumes dependency, which is a method of evil economy, thus, evil society may be dependent upon good society. The ultimate end of evil society is desolation, as such, I prescribe evils to be a temporary dysfunction in the world, a problem that is beset to man that he must understand and accomplish not the moral choice, but also the Processionalist choice that evil is dependent, a temporary deficiency in men that is a current conflict in mans universal challenge, as a stage of progress. In today's business, evil men are forced to comply with the rules of business, or they are criminals. If they comply with business, then how are they guilty? If they begin with criminality, and then move into regular business, do they remain criminals? Or if they have not offended as criminals, but they think to do so, are they criminals? Thus, when are they evil, and when are they not. The answer is when they choose to be evil, and when they choose to be good. The man that takes part in business after being a criminal is maintaining that he does not participate in society according to the established order. Instead, he thinks that the origin of his money and his business is against society, and that he must satisfy his evil pleasures in knowing that he has his settlement in society by evil origin. This allows him to understand that he is a renegade in society. So, we have conformity of evil men to legitimate work, but with some form of pledge or covenant with evil, in that they see the benefit of goodness in its prosperity. However, society may shape a person, and some criminals are not shaped by society, and they think that is gain. It is true, that society is not normally to shape people, and they think that they have averted societal plight, and have lived like aristocracy. The ultimate end of evil must not betray work itself, unless it is true anarchism.

The devils may offer realms and kingdoms, so their currency is profitable for wealth and luxury, and as stated, where there is knowledge, there is order. So I find an evil economy that understands the need of truth, honesty and hard work which conform to a greater need or survival. To these kingdoms I will denote the identification of conservatism rather than liberal thought, that they are principled rather than impetuous, and yet still their work is not counted. There is an overarching error in regard to profit and morality, whereas underneath the authority of criminals is the generation of slavery.

3.7 Conclusion of Error

Error in the hands of people, is used for destruction. Error is a destructive force, and is used to destroy, erode, and expose a dominion. The ruins of a civilization may stand as a testament that it was not destroyed by men. However, the traces of error and destruction, whether by men or nature, illustrates the marks of death, regret and falseness, anarchy, destruction, and it is a sign of deficiency.

4. Success

4.1 The Way of Success

Success is an accomplishment, a requirement in the cosmos that understands inherent meaning in power, it is the satisfactory required/met progressions that bring capability and advancement. Success is processional because he may move forward in cosmic event when he has proven that he has met its requirements. In this regard, success is seen as a gateway in Processionalism because he passes through a portal by reaching the requirements of succession. This brings mastery of circumstance (power in the cosmos) and of self (empowerment in cosmic ability).

Power will govern with total control over its sphere of dominion. Power will always select what is more advantageous; it will elect that which is superior in knowledge to bring succession, and knowledge is a sign of great dynamic potential, so that success is the knowledge of more powerful things, this is Processionalism. To succeed is to maintain, or to increase power. Power is the method of rule, in every aspect because it establishes powers' precedent. In every aspect, power may afford for what is needed, and power is necessary for all things. Ultimately, power is supreme. Power is in all of the politics, and it is behind every political reason, including justice, and all of the ways in the cosmos that power may be. The way of ascension is with power, and many will rise in power due to Immortalaeism. Success is natural, as it is the advancement and it is the way of life human life. Being greater at life is the same as being more successful, and this is our pursuit throughout all of life, so that we are accomplished and that our skills and talents bring us confidence in their execution for what we must do in life. This accords to knowledge and order, and it is demonstrated with greater power, and greater apprehension of the logic and understandings of the concepts in the realm of the concepts and the great schemata, and all that applies in the universe in order to act, and perform the possible acts of men. This accords with ascendance, which is the refinement of knowledge, which indicates graduation, which is Processionalism.

Success is advancement of being a portal that opens in Processionalism because of cosmic understanding, a gateway. Temporally, to meet the accordance of standards is profitable for needs and understanding, however the advancement of being is the epitome of success. Individual successes are profitable, and success of being is the manifestation of greater cause and purpose. Success will afford advancement of any type, so to succeed is to be permitted advancement, and advancement to what is next. The next thing in success is gathering to an overall accomplishment to move forward though a portal (to proceed). What is next is dictated by the constructs of reality, and thus there is reason, and there is the universal code of progress. Processionalism, in its successes will bring us to our chosen future, our destiny, in the way that the universe has dictated that we shall succeed, progress, and understand, in accordance with its orders and ordinances. Power itself is my guide and proof that all such things are true, and in accordance with universal understanding. Following the way of advancement is also following the way of Power. Processionalism is the way of power, and of understanding different powers and how they function. Advancement of being will increase overall power and understanding, but individual increases in power may only enhance a few things. The success of power in its potential is not normally understood, that is, to what end he may understand power and 'become'. In Immortalaeism, he may be a god or an immortal, it is power that provides advancement, and to know a way of power is to know a confidence that he will understand that power is leading him and drawing him into the future.

4.2 Power in Advancement

Increase in power in advancement indicates that there is an enhancement in what is produced. Production comes through the method, and it is in the method that we may locate the source of an increase in power. But why? What is within the worlds orders that indicates that when the method is advanced, that there is an increase in power? I shall say then that all dominion is measured in the metaphysics, and that to eclipse the dominion more quickly means that he possesses greater understanding, and that he can make the domain elementary in its simplicity by the way in which he understands. By such method, he has greater power because he has greater mastery over a domain, and herein within mastery is the method that brings an increase in power, it is the way of power which I have elucidated. I have briefly handled the idea of perfection, and perfection is attributed by the idea of function, and function is qualified by purpose. I shall say then that when the function of something is accomplished that its purpose in fulfilled, and that this is the perfection of a work, and that the greater the work, the greater the power, and that as knowledge increases, the work becomes more powerful. I shall then say that advancement is as progress, and that power is my natural way of life, for I desire to advance, and to near and accomplish perfection, which inducts me into greater power and understanding. What is advancing, but that it is from success to graduation, which tends to progress, which is unending. To advance signifies accomplishment, where what is preliminary contains the basis, that is, constituent aspects that are substantive in the respect of being understood in antecedence before an advancement and reformation of knowledge.

4.3 Absolutism of Advancement

Advancement is necessary, and it has broken the chains of life. Advancement is combined with inertia in space and time, and we always advancing, or we are inert. Advancement means that I must express the full meaning of my being, in time. Advancement contains learning and succession, and that his advancement is equal to his achievement. Advancement means life-knowledge and wisdom, and also power from understanding. Advancement is all that he could ever design for himself in life to have, because he does not know anything else but advancement. In the mind, advancement is the only thing that matters. He advances by power, by accumulating accomplishment. Inertia is related to death, and advancement is related to life. Advancement means that is he progressing with the divine, because he is working with the great schemata that is persistently controlling the mediums of that which is happening because of fates grand order. Advancement is the object of success, to proceed in one's own purpose.

5. Prophecy/Fate / Destiny

5.1 Introduction to Prophecy

Prophecy is a gift that allows people to tell of the future. It also allows the interpretation of spirits, symbols dreams, prescient history, people, places, the past, and of heavenly things. It allows the interpretation of events according to truth. I first had a prophetic experience when I was eighteen. I was taken out of my body, above the world, and I was shown the battle line upon which a war between good and evil would begin, and time fell away from me in the world, I was half dreaming in lucid prophecy, without any notions of time or space, I had a first encounter with both god and the devil, on an ethereal plane, and I was asked if I would sit down and play a cosmic chess game. I could see a great hall, and there were other gods, and they had become aware of me at this time. The chess games was separate from the vision, and the vision was private. In the vision, I was unctioned to choose between good or evil. I decided which aspect of the war I would take, and I began to study religions, in order to write a religion, Immortalaeism. As having prophesied accurately many world events, without a singular error, I will give an evaluation of the gift of prophecy.

5.2 Normative Prophetic Experience

The event is the electric power of our Immortalae prophet, sensing and relating to other powers in the heavens. For instance, in regular prophecy, I shall say that a prophet is under his god, and that he speaks and acts of his god and on behalf of his god. In this case, the prophet has a channel of communication open to his god, and the prophet sufficiently understands/is empowered by his god, that his god may use him as a instrument because the prophet is living in the same power as his god, that is, the two are "living by the same spirit", so that they exhibit and receive the same kind of experience in the world. So, a prophet being under his god is to say that they have the same electricity, the same power. The electricity that the prophet has is, let me say, red, and his god has red electricity, and the electricity communicates all of the understanding of the god to the prophet by electromagnetism to the prophet's mind. We may also say that the red power, or electricity, interacts/is the intelligence of the god, thus when it is cast out by the prophet, he reads the response that his god would receive by interacting with other power in the world. The future and the eventuality of the god and of the prophet is determined by the way the red power interacts with the world and with other power and electricity. The power that one has is the power that one will use to interact with the world, by the same rule, if a god dies, then the power of that god dies, and so will that prophet's ability, so long as it depends upon god, and so will that prophet. The power cast out finds all of the necessary ends of the intelligence of that god, and thus, the prophet understands before time, what would happen if his god, or if he, interacted in the places where he sends the electricity. People are always changing because of the way they need to interact with the world, sometimes in response to the world, at better times, to predestine a response. When someone takes on a new god, or new overhead in their lives, they change the power of their life in the ordinances of the Heavens, and what happens to the overhead will happen to them, and their end will be the same. Prophesying a world event is similar. If someone can prophecy a world event, without any devices, it means that they have a world power with them. If someone may determine what will happen around the world by prophecy, then that person has world power, because they are 'casting out electricity to the ends of the earth in order to understand what occurs'. In the event that such prophecy arises, such a prophet should assume that he is capable of world concourse. This prophet is capable of representing his faction to the nations of the world.

The problem with prophecy is that it does not convey the things necessarily that are desired, but rather desultory things, or occasional things, this is the historical view. At times a prophet may look and force his way into a subject, in order to see what he may read, but the idea usually draws the concept that the origination of the prophecy must be according to a progenitor or a power that is different and is not the prophets own will. I believe that the case of my prophecy, that I prophecy after my own 'electricity', and that this electricity favors me after my own will, such as a life force, or an energy which surrounds me, and that it is a universal force, and a guiding force that informs me of many things. False prophecy would be interpreted as evil prophecy to Immortalaeism, that is, prophecy with a false will, or a false god. In this, they come from a will that is contrary to the will of myself, it is a will that I find false in presiding against me in the universe. However, in the case of false prophecy, there it the event where a plan of evil is unctioned, and as such, goodness would never listen to their prophecies or their will, or anything from them as viable, yet the evil plan has counted its works, and it has counted how its power must be effective in order for the prophecy to come to pass. If it is against the truth, then it is false, even if it does come to pass. As the creator of this religion, I convey the notion that dualisms are true, such as good and evil, and light and darkness, but that Power itself is ultimate and universal. It is good to understand that power exists and matters only, fundamentally, and it is good to understand that power will rule the Earth, but it is better to receive the promise of power, which I have, and it is better to understand the differences of power in the world, and to conquer our enemies. The Edifice of the Provocation of all other powers in the world will rise after my revelation of Power, and they will say that they should not wage war with my edifice of Power, and that it should not be challenged, and that in conquering, my people are justified, and a sign shall appear in the heavens, and the Earth shall be given to my people, and they will rule it.

5.3 Manifest Predestination

Prophecy reaches into the scouring of the heavens and into the future, it seeks remnants of understanding with which it can understand that which has taken place in the heavens, over and above the Earth, in relation to it. We say that earthly powers are not heavenly, but that the celeste above the earth is a first order, and that the earth is a second order. But what is the creation of a wave of water or a beam of lightening in its essence except that it is something divine in origin. I relate my prophecy to the power of my being, and Powers that govern over events. It is evident to me that one may view prophecy as relating to electricity, I display this as a metaphor, or symbol. In electric events, the heavens scour the earth to understand where lightning may strike. In prophecy, the prophet searches the powers of the heavens to understand events with greater calculation, necessary inculcations, and eventuality in order to understand what will occur according to a power that has predominance in prescient certainty over a circumstance, in order to interpret and convey as actuality before present truth. I call such prophecy Manifest Predestination. The prophecy has manifested itself in the heavens, and its actuality is certain over a projected future. It is like fate locating the reality that all other possible outcomes are false, and only one is true, thus predestined. In this, fatalism is used by the prophet because he has accessed fate, and he understands that inevitable events will occur.

Thus, in cause of self as Immortalae, astrally, she must align her purpose, and her truth, and her circumstance, and her relationships and her beliefs and then in meditation she will derive clarity and centeredness, which will bring furtherance in cause. She will then pass through the monotonous spirits of 'Toxycant', which are false possibilities that have deluded her so that she will not achieve great cause in exchange for a lesser existence, which alleviate her of her vocation and the life of her true self. The balance of Toxycant is a solution of various spirits and causes, and that the proper balance is organized in Immortalaeism, and that she must alleviate herself of dementia from the false notions and spirits of the world. To bring life and power to oneself is health and fullness, it is progress and truth and excellence. We will not accept deficit spirits of poverty and diminishment.

In the Immortalae, a right cause will dissolve the barriers of inhibition and derived destiny in certainty of cosmic purpose. This will be achieved through mediation and centeredness, so that the Immortalae will be in the first place of the true life of self. The energy of their wellness and inner peace derived through meditation, will develop into the energy of their power Coae, through being, and this in turn will develop into the focus of ability, and the ability of power.

5.4 Prophecy and Immortalaeism

In Immortalaeism, a prophet will not have a god, he will learn to channel world and universal powers according to his own power, and in universal powers, he will become Eternal and Immortal and they will become gods. They will possess great knowledge and relics, they will be involved in concourse, and they will be the elite of the world. In Immortalaeism I will school my prophets to prophecy at will, and to understand the intricacies of prophecy, and to take clairvoyance into various studies and furtherance's of the gift. I will teach my prophets to understand symbols, dreams, interpretations, and I will have them process Concept-Art with reality and I will begin to construct a picture of celestial, worldly and universal representations into an organization of knowledge that will search the fabric of life and existence. They will become fates and prophetic gods and immortals, with a wealth of knowledge that will make them exceedingly wise.

5.5 Fates Grande Order

Transference is the mode of equating, and inference is the science, or equation or mode of implying/graduating. Transference will extend a domain within its original power, and inference will bring new understanding. There is only one other property besides transference and inference in the universe, which is to act from a will. Like a river that flows throughout all time, our rivers will maintain their course, until we change them in accordance with our wills. The shores will stay the same, they are not moved by our wills, they are bound in transference and inference. Fate has a Grand Order, and it understands our ends before we meet them. Fates Grand Order has the Dream, it has the Force of Will, and it has the Actuality of the Eventuality of what we design for ourselves. It has the dream because it understands our possible futures, it has the force of will, because it realizes our wills in the world and universe, and it has the actuality of eventuality of what we design for ourselves, because it has the design, and we also have the design. In the structuring of the cosmos, the cosmos generates order that permeates throughout, in order to predict this order is the knowledge of fatalism, and fates. It is mastery with contentment and inner peace because we understand the movements of the spirit of the Earth and the power of its constant heavens. We understand moving in progress or regress by what is negative or positive to work and growth. We understand the world and why it progresses or regresses, and we begin to understand fate. We begin to understand why circumstances form in the world, and we begin to understand the oracle, the meeting place of the worldly and the heavenly powers, within circumstance. We arbitrate, and we see powers such as justice, leaving its pattern of power in the world, according to virtue and vice. We understand the difference of the power of the good, and its divorcement of evil, and we understand the constancy of the heavens, and that earthly powers are beneath us for habitation.

5.6 Fate and Destiny

Where destiny is in accordance with immutability, as I say, with the truth of our lives, so that destiny is what we meet in the Universe, when we accept for ourselves the truth of knowing ourselves, and selecting the truth of our lives at every junction, and we will see the conference of the universe establish for us an eventual end, and a story that the Universe affords a place, where the elements involved in our lives and wills will play for us, so that we may meet the procession of our lives after the truth of our lives, and Universally, in a grand theatre, the conflict of powers will meet under the balances and harmonies of dualistic and Primordial and divine universal interplay, and after the play of Fates Grand Order. Fates Grand Order plays a role in this, by providing the un-baptized approach to life, where every decision marks a path of future eventuality, but destiny is baptized/cleansed by divine truth, but both share the meeting places of where they see power for themselves, the gathering of individual beginnings and ends, no matter where they have come from. In destiny, I understand that in the progression of life and times and wills, that the divine of the Universe will be invoked by the grandeur and the height of destiny, sanctioning that the incipience of our wills in prime cause, is divine as well. We may say that, taken to the invocation of the high households and powers of the universe, that in the requirement of destiny, that the necessary causes of where ourselves and lives bring us, may be into the universal displays and theatres, as we ascend to great heights. Destiny is the truth of self, in the greater cosmos and universe, because of the truth of being itself. It is impossible to meet the destiny of someone else, except that a rivaling power may intercept him on his destiny. Destiny is to harmonize with a great cosmic power in the essence of the verity of the path of a single life, and to understand its assurance and belonging, in that it was forecasted he she would meet such markers and destinations of success, and the confirmation is within her being, that beyond her own will and power, that she is seeing the masterfulness of universal power and destination.

5.7 Accepting Destiny

Destiny is what I recommend for Immortalae. The first rule of finding destiny, is to know thyself, and to force your will from your knowledge of self, into the world, and to begin to realize who you are in the world, what commonly happens to you, what happens to you all of the time. Through meditation, which I also advocate for Immortalaeism, you will realize that many people of the world are of lesser problems and different problems, working through lesser equations in the world, that challenge them. When learning to be Immortal, you will find that by meditating on the material I have provided for Immortality, that you will be required to locate the knowledge of self, and by accepting self, you will overcome many elementary life's questions in the world, that many do not overcome, even before death.

Destiny is derived through focus and the centre of one's personal truth and being. She must understand the harmony of all of her causes in life and her own personal mission of veritas (truth), and not to abandon her purposes that are confirmed to her own spirit and being; and unite them in one understanding of what she does in the world. When she is no longer divided into many places in the world, she will be able to see the fullness of her life from a certain point, and in this is where she must collect herself in order to move to the next place in progress. The totality of her meditation is required so that she can understand the harmony of her being with its available cosmic energy and force. This is power, and it should come as power that should bring a more powerful image and cause to herself. In this, power will make her a more powerful self, and a progressed self through Processionalism. Understanding is key, in that she must study to understand how to create furtherance and promotion within her own being, maturity. Maturity and to centre are the most indispensable aspects here, without them is only confusion (as both maturity and a centering are necessary for processional movement). After Maturity and Procession come new life and also Higher Calling. This is a cyclical pattern to progress where new aspects of life are generated through the accuracy of knowing and centering of self, with maturity, leading her to her higher callings that are a part of the truth of the power of her inherent being. Accepting destiny leads to the true oracle of her life, and when she has a uniform grip on her power in veritas, she will begin to create a singularity from which she will be assured of the circumspect aspect of the wholeness of her own life, and it will create a singularity. From the singularity, she will begin to manifest destiny, and she will begin to see what that cosmos has for her, in accordance with the Immortalae Icon of her astral self. The path of destiny is to be trusted in, and the faithless will not know destiny, and they will not know Immortalae, or their purposes in the Universe. They are divinely accepted and trusted with great powers, they are kept in the immortal balance of mankind, chosen as the governors of divine and universal power and are meant to inherit the powers of the universe, and they are kept safe astrally in the world, by being known and reserved in their true character and essence, apart from change, in the nebulas and spaces of astrology. Their inherent destiny is to learn to fight and universal powers (representing), and also to train and be together in the likenesses of one another, as Guardians and the keepers of universal power and its ultimate technology as a universal element of their possession. They are the embodiments of differing powers and schools of thought and power (Toxycant). They are not special in the Earth, more than another man, but they are unique in themselves as men and champions of power, fighting, heroism, immortality, eternity and the way of fighting, through which they must receive the fullness of their powers, because they accept that they will become an Immortal Immortalae because they believe in its verity, so that she can be fulfilled in the reality of her being and purpose, united in the expedience and fulfillment of its reality from day to day. The Immortalae will be as gods of war.

The Paths of Destiny is that the fulfillment of Immortlaeism is the fulfillment of destiny, not only for the Immortalae, but includes furtherance for any man or woman intellectually for progress as well in Processionalism. The notion of Toxycant, and the intellectual apparatuses of Immortlaeism provide furtherance in philosophy and intellectual progress and tools that are philosophical, so that they can become the fulfillment of what the truth of their intellectual endeavor may be. Thus, the greater use of my writings will further universal spiritual and philosophical aspects of understanding, 'to *know* and to *proceed*'. The power books are to be used as books of virtue with intellectual tools for use. They are the said aspect of dominion and power, and are profitable as the complete dialogue of power from Immortalaeism (Power I, II, III, and Empire), and the Immortalae books are written for the benefit of the spiritual aspect of Immortalaeism. (The books of Immortalaity the Universal Way of Power, and the Way of the Immortlaeism.)

6.   Reality/the Universe

6.1 The Metaphysics of Power (Revisited)

In order to pass a power, he must acknowledge the higher unifying concept and its law-table in order to understand if he is beyond, or over that power so that he does not need to accept it. In the cosmos, we usually see powers divided into dualities, unless we provoke a neutral element. It is not occasional that we would see a third aspect, which would make it a trinity, or different sets of powers that work in relation. It is in demonstration that he must ascend in power, and that he must overcome a power. This comes by full agreement with the power itself, and with its higher unifying concept. The higher unifying concept is in a greater network of tables and concepts that govern powers. For example, good and evil are attached to his morality, his religion, his ethics and so forth. But his spirituality is in coincidence with the powers that are in conformity with his being as a man, and he may not need to accept every sphere of power. Power channels through the law-tables, it is underneath these laws and tables that power is found, coursing through them in channels. Do not err, do not be of double mind, these are the teachings of power. These are the teachings of Immortalaeism that make sense in order to progress as a martial artist. He will understand how to accomplish great energies because he understands Immortalaeism. In Immortalaeism, there nothing else except power and its teachings, and there is nothing except martial arts, and its teachings, and there is nothing except immortality and its teachings, and there is nothing except heroism, and its teachings.

He will find the course of power by investigating the law claims of the powers that are in the world, and how they channel from their spheres into his being, because the powers are in the world. He will learn to graduate as a student of power, questioning and accepting how power is to come to him. There are centers where power is concentrated that he must reach, and learn to access. He must be the one that understands the mastery of his circumstance, and not many things. The evidence of his will being centered on his selection will produce a result from the cosmos, and he can change his life. He understands how life changes because he realizes that power is available to him. Above these law tables is an ultimate law table, which is what is available to him in power as a man, because of what man is. He must decide what the world is to him, and through which spheres of knowledge he accepts that he is learning from. Some spheres matter, others do not because of what is superior.

What is time in respect of power? Let us say he is drawn by power and consumed by it. Power is usually the imputation that marks what time means to us. If he becomes twice as powerful in his domain, then he can perform twice as much work in the same period of time. If he becomes consumed by power, does he evade time, and does being enfolded in power mean that he has everlasting life, because he has all things at once? Mortality becomes less because power brings revelations of knowledge and simplicity to the works of men. If he is possessed by power in an eternal way, so that power intends that he should live forever, the aspect of time is diminished, and for all of powers' benefits he is augmented. The dying will is reduced in power, dying men have no power. Power is the greatest thing to him, because if it wills that he is not dead, then he will have everlasting life, it is the belief of Immortalaeism that virtue and power and Eternal life are ways of finding one another. It seems this is the case, because power can change what time means to a man because of what he must accomplish. Power forces what is 'next'. In this regard, power has an affinity with time, because it is in control of the deliverance of what is adjacent in time.

6.2 Power in Series

Power that is not expended theoretically, the source of power itself and where power returns to, is where power does not expend itself in time, and it rests eternally in its potential. A quanta of power may be the power that it would take in order to perform a task from its beginning to its end. This is also the power of a talent in terms of performing works, and quality of works. The power of charged energy itself is only energy, except when it is converted through a series that manipulates its usefulness and expends it and changes it into an energy that bears the representation and production of the field of the series. For example, electric power will convert to whatever medium can master it. Where talent brings a finished result, and the end of powers' usefulness in the series was the mastery of power itself. What is charged energy, power itself in its electric form and domain, what is power in the universe? Power is the way of all things, and without power, there is nothingness. Power is not what something is necessarily, except power itself, but the identity of a thing itself is the representation of its metaphysical and invisible essence and identity. Power is the way of expression, and power is necessary for life itself, and existence in the physical universe. A god has many dependent forms, and power comes from the place where all forms are as one, and power itself understands all forms and expressions because it must fill them, they are known to it. All forms are known to power, because they operate by power. Power contains the polarity and the magnitude of the universe, and power is the key to understanding universal expression, because power arrives at the universes potential in order to create. Power is in the beginning and the end of all events universally. Power is in time, and power understands dimension and change. Power understands being. In Immortalaeism, the aspect of being is to tie a knot of immutability so that he will find eternity in his own being, and he will understand energy and power, so that he will always be full of power, he must understand the ways of eternal and immortal life, and he must venture into this commitment and shed the ways of the world in order to grasp its reality. He must understand the construct of the spiritual, and the way of ascension of being, and he must become immutable so that his power is formed into in the infinite, and that his life will fill the world with infinite possibility. There are many places that he may be, except truly only one, which is the aspect of being that comes through the physical matrix and representation of life. Life understood as a matrix of inferring design are series of codes and in order to understand a code, he must have at least met the understanding of that code in his own being. This pertains to domains and spiritualities, and it is spiritualities because the domains are made in the construct of the spiritual. This is a much grander view of life than wealth and riches and poverty. In this understanding is his spirituality, and the potential of his choosing and his understanding and the implications of his intelligent being. Ideologies are only aspects of spiritual powers and their explanations in absolute terminology and litigation.

In terms of humanity, power must find a place to rest in the being of a man, so what accommodates power so that it may rest in great potential? Power resides in what is capable of holding it, in the utmost of its power. Power is demonstrated in a dam in the redirection of a channel, and power is demonstrated in a higher dominion that can control a lesser dominion. Power is demonstrated by great intellect and great force from a will, and great resistances. Power is demonstrated in the modules of logic and inference, streaming and moving the parameters of reason to suit what is universally acceptable, the way of universal power. Thus, power meets above the way of the universe with the reason of the universe itself, and why event happens the way it does (occurrence). This occupies the notion of separation itself, and that which is separate and distinct and why there are different powers. As in metallurgy, I may pour two metals of equal mass into a channel, but perhaps I am supposed to acquire twice as much of only one of them, because to mix two of them together will produce a brittle solid metal. I must select the purity of my duality, my logical parameters and the flow of my intelligence, and in the end, the mixture that I have that reasons with universal logic will produce a result in the end that denotes approval/succession. Thus, power operates by the flow of power, through logical modulators, in the intelligence of knowledge and understanding. Success is determined by where power finds itself after all logic and argumentation is finished, and determines the result of life's choices. The greatest use of logic and power then, is not to mix ideology and theory incorrectly, and not the damage the purity of the concepts, and in this, not only will he be more powerful in the end, but he will be rewarded with passage to the next sphere of understanding, and if he damages the concepts he may be struck by power.

6.3 Spiritual Boundary

Powers are in the universe, and they may be accessed by endorsing the dominion of a power. The power must accept the form and presentation of the individual, and it must allow him through its 'gates'. The endorsement of a power comes by full representation of a power. To contradict that power, is to oppose it, which is to lose power in that dominion. By understanding the implications of certain core truths of a power, the proper conduct and reasoning's may accord with an acquired dominion. Many do not understand what they do, and what they do, they understand that they do it with beliefs that are not held in dominion. They are in fact acting in the power of a state or a dominion, but they understand nothing of why they have any power at all. They are understanding that in the corollary of their bracket which is in their mind which accords with foundational beliefs, that they are using a few understandings that they have gathered over time, which are regulating their behavior, but all of these things that come together for them are in place by dominions which have taken time to endorse these individuals, and they understand that they receive from a dominion, they are like mercenaries, rather than heirs, and they do not understand where their power comes from. They have met a spiritual boundary.

Many nations have a personal way of displaying power, and their power is shaped over time, by additions to the realm. As I said, that power is my politics, I interpret such methods of the way that nations display their representation, and also the full scope of what a nation is/does, and I understand the power of nations. Thus, in thesis and anti-thesis, I view nations struggling with one another, and I see their methods of conduct, and I simply see power, and their allegiances to power. I see that in a greater representation of power, that a nation will become more effective, more intelligent, and a greater power will rest with its identification with the source of their power and identification, and I see that in understanding their source of power and representing it to a further degree, that they will properly understand the extent of the dominion that they are inheriting for developing a nation after the form of behavior the thought patterns that they have used in order to become who they are.

6.4 The Universe

The universe is power. The beginning and the end of all things is power. There is nothing but power. All things that we see are only representations of power, and in the ethereal/metaphysical/realm of the concepts, the full architectonics of power are visible, and since power will always select what is more advantageous, so also is the future of what will become of us. In the Earth we grow with power and we decide on power in our ways. We are a people of power, navigating possibilities with life and death. The ability of ability is power, as I have said, and all things that pertain to the excellence of progress, in that all is progress, is the rise and the fall of powers, for which reasons we may search out and understand, and we may understand principle and utilize the powers of governance in accordance with our wills, for in the sequence of masteries, we find that we are closing in on the apprehension of the problem of Finality, which is constancy and satisfaction in the knowledge of self, and satisfaction in one's ability in the universe. The method of immutability does not always mean that I will never progress, but I will progress after the affinity of my own intelligence. I will die, if I do not understand the problem mortality, but I may not die, if I attempt to become what is everlasting in the identification of self.

The universe is power to me, and I understand my place in it. All temporal living, I have forsaken, there is nothing in this Universe for me but the immortal knowledge of myself in immutability and constancy, where my will lasts forever as a real power in which I represent a real dominion in the Universe and I convey its intelligence in whatever I do.

"I never actualize what I say, and what I do, I mean only as long as others are providing a sense of self security. I mean that in life, I have accomplished a strong sense of responsibility, because they have afforded me a place of assurance in their organizations. My knowledge is founded in my sense of security, and because of all of this, all that I do I do not actually do, and it is all temporal. I am the pawn of a cosmic chess game, and my consequence is my actual being, but my intelligence provides me only with what dominion I ascribe to serve. My consequence is what you will be if you act upon me, but ultimately, I do not know this myself, unless I understand that that is the only power I have as a defense in the world. I am a servant according to my intelligence, for I do not have the power to rule, for I possess no foundational knowledge, and no one will teach me because I am not worthy of education, for I possess no courage, and I possess no real purpose. In the universe, the consequence of my existence is that I will perish according to my will, in service to a dominion, but not ruling in a dominion". The elements of universal powers that are involved in this man's life are rudimentary. There is nothing divine in this man's place in life, and nothing of great worth. Universal powers of divinity will, as I have stated in 'Power', will notice the interchanges of a life when the greatness of that life and its exemplary actions reach the heavens. To remove such translucent language, in order to make these things clear, I will say this:

The universe will reward that which is worthy in the reflection of dominion. "What is the Processional value of the relation of the universe to dominion?" Rulership is an associate with the ultimate and total understanding of a realm and realms. Thus, it is the essential knowledge of a power, it is the location of where power will come from itself, if a realm is compatible with that power, and that power will supply the life and effectiveness of a nation, a country, a city, or people. So we shall say that the Processional value of the universe in relation to a dominion is that I shall understand the power that I use as much as the power understands itself, and if I understand only a fraction, then I may act under accordance to that power, but only in a fraction, and not in the whole.

The truth of relation of a power to itself is that the power will understand itself, and it has a place in the universe. Power will reflect that it has won a place in the universe, and it understands how it relates to other powers, and it understands its place. Where does power get its place? It obtains its place in origination, as a Prime in itself, and it relates to other powers as derivatives. How is a prime formed? As a man, I choose to be a principle in itself from my denial of other powers, and I find my place. A prime is formed by the power of necessitation and creation, which makes a place for all that is logically necessary, by the power of inference and transference, they are made. As thus, the formation of a power is inaugurated, and a great transference is made, and new battles and arguments and problems will begin with the powers that are already formed, and they will conjecture and prove the relation of the new power to others in the Universe. This is the formation of all argumentation and of all of the problems of skepticism and debate, in that the origination of them all lies in the powers from which they derive from, so that they may prove their significance, they will understand these powers, and they will believe in accordance with them, in that they may prove their significance in the orders of the universe. The orders and the significance is that all of the powers will provide a product in their efficaciousness, and they will always have their place, and they shall always prove the truth of their creation, and they will always have the same order, which their significance comes from. Significance is a word that accords with the truth of relation from being and cosmic order, thus we shall say that significance is derived from order, and order from the original position of a power.

The progress of progress is that the selection of how something is achieved is already given in the universe. It must mature, it must accept higher opinions which are difficult which must be founded by great achievement. Why should it be this way, that progress is based in success, according to order and dominion? It seems that he cannot fall below death, and there is no other way in the universe, so he must move in the way of the world. He cannot escape that there is more in the world, but he cannot reach it, because the lessons of his circumstance are teaching him that he must comply with the way of eternal life, because he does not understand death. Death is one escape for *him,* it allows him to think of time and life differently. After the power of his will, beneficence and it is procession, in that he will become something greater than he was, and he will change, but he will not forget all that he has accomplished.

Success is the way of power, it is universal, and it is the way of all things for man, and it depends what it may be, upon what his achievement is. Success is to know a way of power, and he will understand power, or he will know nothing at all in the world and cosmos. I am a master of power because I have taken its lessons. I see many powers in the heavens, and that I am a power because of my representation and understanding. The universe holds my teaching.

6.5 Reality

"I was once a great man of concourse, and I understood reality, and thus, I understood my place, and I was afforded a place in international business, because I understood the reality, the principles of the world that create the world as it is, in which I live, and I was given a place to succeed after my own talents, and I became a leader after my own intelligence, and I made a place for myself in the world, and I knew that it would not be moved, and for that I was wise."

"I was a king that never moved for any man. In my place, I understood the objectives of my people, my family, I understood the kings before me, in a long decadency, and I understood our science, the ambition of my family in the sight of all knowledge. I ventured beyond the limits of what is normally done, and I became a marvel, and so did my regime. I found a place of originality, and to venture after my knowledge is to follow after my people and my family, and thus, in forging a path of progress in the world, I have won a place in the histories of the world, and my significance is of a high order."

"I was a guard, with the understanding of this world, and the next, and the next, and I found a place of belonging, and so I served not as the highest, but as a guard, with the understanding of many kings, and I became a guard over civilization. I had the knowledge of a sphinx, and I governed in the place of those with which I found accordance after belief. The problem of my life was that I could not find a place of security, until I found those that shared my place in the Universe. I was the first of enlightened society, and for that I am wise."

Reality is the dominion of the world. The construct of what this Earth is, the extension of this world to survival, to the ends of the universe, and to the next world, and to our afterlife. Reality is the project of inference and transference, in which we understand what is logical, what is sensible, what is pragmatic, what is reasonable, what is virtuous, what is high, what is actual and what it is to understand ourselves in this world as people. For we determine what is low, what never happens, what is vice, what is unreasonable, what is insensible and what is illogical, in accordance with the supremacy of our wills.

In Concept-Art, we see the confluence of ideas represented after a dream-like state. In Concept-Art, we see the relation of things after our own creation, and we explore the progressions of relations after a science of what we understand to be reality, the boundaries of reality, and thus, the images and the relations, and thus, the Concept-Art is real, and it would be, if we ever encountered it in the real world. Reality is similar to Concept-Art, it is the relation and the progressions of ideas and the truths of things, so that we may see the consequence of our beliefs, after the truths and boundaries of the world. Here is all wisdom, all wisdom is that everything will eventually end after the truths of relation in accordance with the truths of reality, as fate. As said, the introduction of new problems and primes will/can change the entire world, after the truth of relation and inference, in accordance with transference.

We see the protagonist in the story of our world, he will be victorious over our enemies, and he will supplant the evil in our lands and in our world, and he will rescue us all, after the apex of the virtues and understandings of our societies. He will be a channel of power and all of our miracles that accord with our power will surround his life, and unction him into victory. He will be an agent of progress and defiance of our darkness's and our evils. We shall say that we found our reality after the significance of various events, various lore, or stories, and we ascribe to such powers as the interpretation of the things that we value that we shall succeed by, and we know the power of that dominion by the proper acceptance of that power, which is likely intrinsic to us from within us, and we do not deny that power, but we see it in accordance with the extent of its dominion, and through Processionalism, we seek a higher standing with those powers, in order that we may know it more fully, and become more powerful after the power that we seek to represent us in our dominions. Such is the making of a power, or a principality, a country, state, nation, or world, or hero.

So, does reality change? We shall say that reality does not change, but we shall say that after the accordance knowledge, we may say that that which was once inaccessible to us, is now within access. We may say then, that the use of knowledge changed for us, once we understood a given principle, or once we found a higher expression for our power, and thus we may say that by such technological advancements, that we found the difference of sciences after progress, which has changed our 'reality', and that in such an imbuement of a given science, that the introduction of a new fragment of knowledge, has made an alchemic difference in the use and understanding of the knowledge of our dominion, so that we may say that reality does not change, but it is either accessible to us or inaccessible to us, which affords us our station in reality.

In Processionalism, it is inferred that by transgressing understandings, that we may fall as a nation or a people, and that we may fall below the antecedence of what affords us our current technology or standing in life, due to the admittance and sanctioning by the powers with which we work. We may say then, that 'we are not worthy of such progress', due to regression, and we may see our society fall below our current standard, and we shall go into decline. We shall say that such implications are serial to us, by the standards of sequentialism, through my Governing Laws of Metaphysics, which at this time as a derivative of my Governing Laws of Metaphysics, I will call Serialism. We may see then that by the standards of progression, that we have defied what is Processional, and we have enabled a serial consequence which is regression, and we thus have defied our own dictates, and we shall fall according to our transgression, and we shall find recovery after the full acceptance and progression in accordance with what we define as progress, and after my first book on Immortalae, that if they are subjects of Immortalaeism, that they have fallen into Sovereignty.

The alignment of powers that one wishes to utilize for his progress will afford him a way of progress. He will become powerful after the initiations of his will, in which he professes and which he understands that he will accept is a rod, or a scepter, or a staff, for the guidance and care of his life. Approval may come, in that by understanding finally the Law of a power, now the instances do not need remembrance. Once the Law is understood, the real power of the Law is released, and one will become more masterful and approved by the power, in order to wield it, after the Law. Thus, he who does this is no longer a magistrate or a lawyer, he becomes an inheritor of the land, the power of the land belongs to him now. Once the Law is understood, he will begin to inherit power as a god of that power. In a picture, he that understands the rays of the sun knows that the rays are the instances of the Law. Once he knows them all, then he understands the circle of the Sun, which is the Law. Once he has accomplished the Law, he becomes a smaller Sun, and in this, he becomes like a god.

What is the prime of such a Sun? There will be written law codes for each type of power, and each law code will be a set of directives, or commandments, and each will be arcane knowledge for those that follow after to find such powers. For Polytheists, we shall say then, that some will go out after a power, and others will go out after other powers, to find the mysteries of all powers, in order to bring them all together after the differences that are within us, and we shall divide the demon from the angel, and the false god from the true god.

6.6 The Astral

The astral in Immortalaeism is open after walking through the astral gate. In Processionalism, he must walk, building his understanding so that it is powerful and correct in all things. As destiny is the truth of self in the cosmic and earthly, Processionalism naturally leads to this end because it builds in truth and universal wisdom. The pyramid of mastery (that is, the representation of triangles) is achieved by understanding Immortalaeism and the conclusions that it brings to understanding the world. Once he has chosen the spheres of his life and his existence eternally, he may balance them and master them in his regular concourse and time. Power, Eternity, Immortality, Heroism (and martial arts), Virtue, Processionalism, The World and Cosmos, Proper Governance of Duties and Responsibilities and Respects and Honors, The Game (Immortalaeism III), Contra (Adversaries), Double-Dragon (the Unfailing, Eternal Friend), Civilization and Guardianship (the Dragon) …Immortalaeism. In this he has mastered a universal place in the world, knowing fully the spheres that are in the world, and accomplishing them responsibly, he is now open to the astral, which is a greater mastery that brings greater power and understanding. This power is so powerful and convincing that when he is immersed in it (when he crosses the astral gate), he will lose his regular sensual nature, and it will be replaced by the potentials of power and its manifestations as a possession of his.

The spheres of the world must be accomplished before graduating to the astral. Man can only rule a given number of spheres that are available to his being, and only in a certain manner, and this derives his spiritual vitality (his life), and also his spiritual kinetic potential (his power). The spheres are: (1) Degree of Perfection, (2) Power, (3) Spirituality, (4) Wisdom, (5) Governances, (6) Spiritual Occupation. Related spheres come next, such as the world itself, being its cosmic and elemental creation in that the man is an intrinsic part of the cosmic earth, and his place in relating to its power. These powers' do not change, and are the universal powers that created the earth. Once he understands the positions and regards of the earth that he must meet, then he may understand the astral by the astral gate. At the gate, the full pillar of the earth is met properly, and the opportunity of the astral avails itself. The astral gate is for the Immortalae, in order to understand cosmic power, and the gifts of eternal living and the greater revelation of being itself.

7.   Serialism

7.1 Introduction to Serialism

One summer I began to study the metaphysics and a priori subjects, and I also began to question complexities of shapes as they relate to the perfection of manmade shapes, their durability and the instance of temporality. On the nature of structures, I began to develop philosophical theories on geometrical shapes and rooms architecturally. Among those developments, I decided that I would begin to develop a philosophy of numbers. In the beginning of this, I considered the numbers one through ten, and I noticed a sequence which I consider to be 'Prime Ordeal'. In a sequence we question and find, "What is next?", and "What is the reason for the Order?". (This is the same as the fundamental aspect of Processionalism, which is to question and to proceed). We see the arrival of an end, but the arrival is completed by the appearance of a number of required events which are next to one another in the realm of the concepts, where the imputation of the first event in the sequence necessitates the second event, etc. Sequence indicates understanding, because when all of the requisite antecedent problems from the first event are completed, an indication of a sequential event in occurrence is realized, and the first event is held completion and in relation to the second event, and the first and the second to the third, etc., and it is these sequences that frame our logic of events and understanding innately. This phenomena is a part of serialism in the astral and in the cosmos, in the planets and their alignments, and also in prime origin. This is the knowledge of creating a world.

7.2 Transference and Inference

'There is no more time…
… 'the force of change itself is moving it into a new state''.

The power of transference is the immutable forward progression of all things, and communication. In transference there is no new knowledge, however, in inference the knowledge base is expanding based upon what principles, truths and understandings can be applied with the given knowledge. The power of inference is the foundation of reason, implication, and understanding, which locates the power which imputes the necessary connection to what is next according to the orders and their cosmic symbol, that is, the hierarchy of knowledge. Thus, there is a logic of all that accords with understanding, which proceeds in a grand order, and there is a power which set all of the orders into motion. These powers are the operators of logic and of the world because it is their truths that govern our experience, and our experience of knowledge. There is no procession without them. Many go here and there in the world questioning and assuming that they have an order in their mind that provides them with success, when they think they understand the consequences of many things they think that they are wise. Changes in decision making hold the greatest power of uncertainty, and it is in the foundation of the world that we have certainty, and that we possess reason. Reason is important, but truth more important because it is not negotiable. To have reason, does not mean that he understands something in the world. It only means that he can negotiate power according to his power of understanding. Consequently, it is in the uncertainty of our wills that we find that our wills and purposes are not aligned with much of the world, and we do find that we are answering questions in the world and bringing ourselves to an eventual end, but only a moderate end because of what one may fathom. The alignment of a will with an eventual end is of greater assurance and decisiveness once one has allocated all of their decisions in life which they are able to make in the world, they will eventually receive from the world a response for the immutable truth they have communicated with their being. The world will only hold a few doors open for him, and the inevitable will take place because the code of his understanding has gone out into the field of the world's knowledge, and he is receiving a response. This means alignment. This means destiny because this is the only option that was available for him in the cosmos and in the real world. In this, they will receive their election, the end of all that their life has meant unto this point in time. After this point in time, they will experience what they have selected as a determinable end to be a new beginning. The world will show them what their life has meant, and what it will always mean. This is obtaining his personal truth from the world. He will have a path of cause and effect that means truth to him, and he will arrive at the end of the world, and at the end of the world, he will know no other possibilities, and all of the negations to available truths and all of the positives to available truth will give him the truth of his identity. Their Prime Cause will no longer reflect the uncertainties they once held, and they will embody a relationship to the world which is above all that they have denied, so that they know a greater truth. At the end of the world, he will know himself and his only possibility, and if he can align himself in new serialism, then he will receive a new sequence of events for himself in life.

This an exchange of A for B, because of the sum (of A) of sequential aspects, the aggregate in its final stage is equal to the acquisition of (B). Transference of A universally, infers a universal B. The processional sequence:

In the life of a person, he chose sequence A, which was:

C->D->E->F->G->H->I->J->K,

Where, since A->B, then A for B

So, A, therefore B, and since A, then B instead of A, thus B in finality.

Thus, I am illustrating a processional leap between the sequence of A, and the graduation to B. So I can say, that in the world, I kept experiencing A, but when I realized B, I elected B instead of A, and now A is no longer effective to me in the world, and I have graduated to B. The sequence A is now inadmissible, and the revelation of B has rendered my life, which was sequence A, now inoperative and ineffective because B is a higher understanding, and institutes a higher sequence. Thus, it is more convenient to me to be immortal rather than mortal, since it is no longer expedient for me to think about dying.

We may say that in any given sense, that A implies B. We may say that in the essence of B, there was the indication of A previously, in order to reach B. So what exactly is the power of inference and necessary cause that institutes that something should follow another? This is another aspect of power. I find that when I segment and differentiate between two things, where one follows the other, let us say, A and B, that when I separate them and inquire into what exactly the power is and does that implied B from A, I find a Higher Principle, or a Higher Sequence, at least, which is above and through the sequence, and I shall call this Higher Principle: Vaul's Theory of Governing Conceptual Law of Metaphysics. I find that when I look past and above and through A and B, that I locate the Principle of Operation, that is, why it functions, that is, the foundation of the world and its ways (ex. survival).

To locate a Higher Sequence is to say that the truth of A and B is an aspect of a greater number of 'truths', or a greater truth, in the relative spectrum of A and B which contribute to a greater equation, an equation which is above A and B, and fundamentally supports the truth of A and B. As I ascend past A and B, I locate that the inferences on the Higher Spectrum are of a Higher Principle. Given the above, I can say that the principle that operates in A and B cannot derive the Above Principle, but that the Above Principle implies A and B. I can also state that ultimately, in the beginning, that independently as elements, there is per se, EXAE (1), and there is DONNE (2), and from EXAE and DONNE there was TRAX (3), and VEXAE (4) and concluding with CENAE (the end), and from the sequence and the conclusion of CENAE, I derive QUAEA (5). We may say that in fully understanding civilization, I understand law, but that in understanding law, I do not understand civilization. Civilization functions by a higher conceptualization than law.

7.3 Vaul's Number Sequence

A) Final Resolution

1. Singular
2. Other
3. Witness
4. Mobility
5. Understanding
6. Conflict
7. Higher Power
8. Council
9. Precision
10. Completion

B) Final Truth

1. Singular
2. Other
3. Witness
4. Mobility
5. Understanding
6. Peace
7. Truth
8. Wisdom
9. Higher Learning
10. Completion / Final Truth

Wherever these numbers are involved with people, these actions will be taken in this order, and the order will not be interrupted. It is a primeval cognition sequence which occurs in people simply by daily activity, or in the orders or nations and states, this pattern is replete.

7.4 Power and Alignment

I perceived singular points in equidistance, like stars in the sky, and I perceived what it means to add a point to another, until the number 10. My objective was to pierce with my intuition into the points representing numbers in order to derive the true meaning of numbers. I found that the essential meaning of what I have derived is primordial to the human race. As the numbers relate to the words, the expression of what is meant in the meaning of the words is deeply polysemous. The ultimate truth behind the sequence is Processionalism. The inculcations of what occurs is inescapable, and the fabric of reality indicates higher powers and universal intelligence. We must know the orders in order to arrive at higher power, and we must accept that alignment and time and power are attempting to cause him to understand their tendencies, which is the indication of what his life in the beginning and in the end, is all about.

The indication is that there are Primes in the world, which are orders that are establishing the Ways of intelligent life. There are events that are required to take place, and in these events there are trials and questions that need to be answered, and there are understandings that must be arrived at, which insist that there is a procession, and an eventuality that is procuring an end to current affairs, that indicates a new beginning. In the deliberation of many understandings, a new understanding occurs which is of a higher principle, which value I will attribute as a prime over the lower schemata. The number sequence which I have presented is a vehicle that will arrive at a Prime, from the view of civilizations overall behaviour. Many lower orders are given place in a political theory, in that all of the argument is heard and given a place, and I will say that if the politics possesses absolution and truth, then some ways of life will be proven incorrect and false, obsolete. This will be done according to my number sequence, and the surrounding primes that are governing over what will become of individuals and societies will, according to their order, provide a denotation and a place according to their understandings, and the manifestation of those judgements and imputations will be evident in the world. Powers that rise and powers that fall due to their conference in the world. Those that have learned to be Good, will arrive at the destination of the Good and the judgements of the Good, and what it means in the astral, and they will have logical and reasonable certainty that as they venture past many of the scepticisms and problems that Good now faces in the world, that the partaking of problem according to our current intelligence and method will be over, and all that is required to understand a graduation to a higher Prime will be necessary to understand a leap in intelligence, and then a new set of principles and governances will be given, and a higher mastery will be achieved. This is (for the Good), the indication of an alignment and that primes are necessitating that he must be on time with its powers in the world, in order to reach the revelation of his way of life.

Dominion is established after primes of power and alignment, and due to transference and inference they will situate themselves from different place to place, according to the ruling power. The alignment of a power is an occasion for its Hero to come into place and understand the power and its cause. This is divination. In the unmanifested are all of the lines and traces and signs and auras. Is it not a clue that a sign comes from the unmanifested? Demonic symbols, symbols of dominion. For example, the power of a dominion has come, but it is inhabited by the architecture which represents its inherent power in brick and mortar, for what that power is astrally. The inhabitation takes on the form of the spirit, in accordance with its accuracy of pristine order and alignment. Creating powers are above in the heavens and earth, and we are meant for this architecture, and for these powers, and they belong to us, and that is confirmed. We do not technologize more than we have spiritual dwelling and provision in the unmanifested. We have these buildings, but until we reach father in understanding power and the cosmos, we will not see new technology (really). The aura is the essence of the spirit, but unlike the heart and the mind in the world, it cannot be destroyed. The aura is the truth of the aggregate of individuality comprised with the ruling spirits of Toxycant. The sign is the effect of the aura. The spirit is the orb of the ruling powers that govern the animus. The life is what one must perform in order to have that spirit. Its astral representation is all of the ruling houses and gates that surround the spirit and aura. They are the earthly and the heavenly gates, and they are the gates of the realm of Toxycant, and its relating astral signs and symbol. The Immortalae will understand Toxycant, and the spiritual world behind the physical world, they will be literate in the spirit and the astrology of the cosmos. The Immortalae will walk from finding the true doors of the realm of the Earth.

8.   Concept-Art

8.1 Introduction to Concept-Art

Concept-Art is useful to us. It allows us to understand, as reason does, the arrival of the end of certain concepts, before they occur, because of natural and universal possibility. Concept-Art is wisdom to us, because we see the in Concept-Art a rule, which is that if someone is attempting to imagine about themselves, they see the Concept-Art circumscribe itself after the reality of the world, so the dream of Concept-Art will always end with the problem of reality, even in imagination. Thus, the 'blessings and the curses' of real life are always evident in Concept-Art. The unwanted, the perverted, the scoundrel, the hero and the favored, the king, the joker/jester, the inventor, the artist, the fallen, the noble, the just, the coward, the fool, the warrior, the evil and the good, they will know as well as in Concept-Art, the real limitations of their dreams. (The necessitations of parameter allude to creation, a construct of Immortalaeism, a reality that implies the orders of heaven influencing Earth.) Concept-Art is also wisdom to us because we are able to freely explore in dynamic intention real concepts and their relationships, and at times, in a story, with a hero who reveals a world of mystery to us. Concept-Art can be surreal to us, because it may bring with it a sense of enigma, as well as stark and truthful 'reality' that bears resemblance to our real lives. It is useful to play with concept-art in order to understand reality. All Concept-Art is built after reality, in the context that it 'could' happen, or that when something happened, this (the Concept-Art) is essentially what it was, in another representation, by transposing the values and arranging an equal world after an equation of scaling and trans-disposition. By understanding symbolism and philosophy, and the grand story of life itself, we may say that one has a pure understanding of Concept-Art, as long as they remain truthful to the reality of the concepts being used, and the truth of character in their portrayals in relation to the symbols, signs and concepts. Concept-art can teach us of realities when the concept of an enemy is made in the design, so that it can display the reality of such propensities in order to prepare a simulation. The concept-game has taken the art, and made it into an arcade, so that he must place himself in the circumstance of the parameters of the reality, and gamble his fortune against the opposition in a manner that conveys realism.

According to my theory, the 'Eye of the Fight', is the focus and lens through which all may be understood by the protagonist, with a truthful outlook of understanding in supposing how events may unfold. We may say that a hero and an anti-hero of equal strength both have an 'eye of the Fight', through which they wield reality after their wills, because they view from beginning to end, how the ensuing battle will correlate, after their knowledge of how they understand life events, and that of their own interpretation of life. This focus of following the story is at times necessary to engage in the event itself.

8.2 Other Worlds. Concept and Symbolism

Concept-Art may allow us to see an equilibrium, where reality, and a fixed Concept-Art realm, are converted by scaling in magnitude and in concept and symbolism, and we may view in a greater scale, the significance of certain events, in that the symbolism will detail to us an understanding of such events in a view that elicits the provocation of significance, because we see the relationships in a scale that provides a view of hidden meaning. At times, the symbols and hidden meanings are deep in the spiritual aspect, yet, the introspection of certain concept-art events are personally compelling, and the meaning of such symbols and events provoke the true essence to us, and they help us to understand superlative truths about our own lives, in the context of other symbols, events and stories, that we may be engaging in the world. The depth of knowledge sometimes produces enigma in the observer. This depth of symbol, sign and concept is derived from stark intellectualism, spirituality, and the truth of life, which is the same as the conceptual being represented in dreams to the sub-conscious, and for the hero, there is the contrast of astral realities. We may thus see the usefulness of Concept-Art, in that it may allow us to see ourselves in the scaling of the Concept-Art, and to interpret that meaning back into our regular lives so that we may see a 'story' that is happening in the real world. We may view a wide range of stories, and interpretations in Concept-Art with proper scaling of worlds in comparison to ours, and we shall see that we have many shades and colors and contours with which we may see the stories and truths of our lives and times. We are at this time, viewing the legacies of the progression of the 'hero', or in any case, the individual of focus, and we are understanding the multifarious vocations and connections of the times which are real to our people in their lives. We see the spiritual context, symbols and powers without modern appearance. We then begin to see that in the Concept-Art world, that if all of our heroes are connected to someone in the real world in identity or possibility, that in the scale of the real world, that we should scc similar stories produced in that person's life, and we shall say that all of the characters of Concept-Art are also all connected in Concept-Art, if we could only be illuminated with the calculation of meetings in the Concept-Art realm, and that it may require a great calculation in order to connect the stories of Concept-Art and heroism together, but essentially, all of the understandings of the different realms and Concept-Art stories are all connected by a great weaving that is done in the Concept-Art world, where on one sheet, all of the different worlds and hero's, losses and victories and enemies are displayed by a great interweaving and wisdom of the world, thus, we may understand how to see the depiction of a true hero in the meaning of concept art.

8.3 The World of Concept-Art and its Interconnectedness

That all of Concept-Art is connected is a mystery to some, but I will explain why all of Concept-Art may be seen in the same tablet, or weaved into the same blanket as a masterpiece of art or as a masterpiece of the loom, as they blend into one another because though their appearance is different, the spiritual requirements are similar in their genesis, and that their times and places, transdisposed into reality, are similar in their duality. When there is legitimacy for a hero to meet with another hero, and share a conflict, it must take place where in Concept-Art, two realms, or worlds, will meet one other, and the heroes must understand one another's conflict and way of life enough to partake in one another's struggle a common meeting place. This must be the case, because in both worlds there is a place that is the same, and a way of getting to that place which from their way of life, he must understand the nature of the meeting because of what it means to them to go to that place. The place is the same to them, because they go there at the same hour. This is the problem of Concept-Art, that heroes will meet forces of darkness and evil together, but that they must reach a point in life where it becomes apparent to the hero that he needs to venture to the place where he unknowingly will meet another hero from another realm. In Concept-Art, their dualisms and their lives are all sharing the same end, and they will see the same fate in the end, in all of the realms of Concept-Art, including electronic games, if our hero's do not win over their enemies.

We shall say all of this in Immortalae, that it is the knowledge of the Immortalae, that these are the stories that we design because these are the problems and the circumstances that we face. That our people see these stories in our world, and live them in reality for, they will see the events and details and components that are against us in the world, and they see what is necessary to combat such forces and elements. We may see then that what typifies certain stories of Concept-Art, that is, what the dispute concerns, may be typified by us and categorized as a type of conflict, and thus, we have a type method of victory if ever that conflict or occasion should rise. Thus, the work of our heroes is replete, and so is their alliance, and we see them completing argumentative, physical conflict, with the combat of evil forces, through a logical sequence and attempt to overthrow a great argument from an opposing evil force. We understand that the genesis of the stories are very different, and the context is a reality in the spiritual aspect and design of the world We shall thus say that in the event of such and such, that we have such and such a resolution according to type case "A", which is located in our stories of heroes. We understand that insofar as a hero has a real burden in the world, that we may see the depiction of heroes throughout time. In the world today, we see a great depiction of heroes, but we do not see the exaltation of non-fictitious heroes, we see the exaltation of Concept-Art. With this, we also see the arrest of heroism, with the exaltation of the justice and governance at the gates of heroism. According to my rule, I then see that in the scaling and transliteration of heroes depicted in society, that those heroes depicted should exist in the world. Will we say that society has no more need for the hero? In the context of heroism, naturally, a hero finds a place of assurance of virtue among people, and he is exalted for such a reason. Naturally, he is doing the works of justice, and for that, he may find conflict in the world. In a great ability to oppose evil, he finds great evil by the same rule, because the fight is the only thing that matters to him, and not society. He understands that society is necessary, but his place is to be in the fight because he is the one that understands it, and he will fight it, because that it what he wants to do. All of those that oppose evil with force must understand that it is not a right of privilege due to a government alone, the government may provide this, and that the instance of justice must usually be taken in order to desire such an affiliation with the government. So the privilege and the first incipience of justice and heroism is with the individual, so that it finds that it is natural in his life to find a great opposition with evils. Thus, the government does not specialize for him to fight evil, and it is his place to find the conflict because he is the one.

The interconnectedness of the worlds is endless in Concept-

Art, and so is conceptualization, symbol and sign because of universality and the possibility of powers and their convergence in the world and streets of society which leaves us with an infinite realm in which we may play, and design our protagonist, and develop a creative world, or realm, after the imagination of what we choose the see in the real world, and if our code of trans-disposition is correct, then we have a virtual reality from which we may view the lives of our protagonists. These are signs of interplay in the cosmic-world that are obvious indicators for the hero that he may meet micro or macrocosms of interface in order to beget his quest to truly face his enemies. By the spiritual architecture and apodictic certainty of the world and society, we will see the emergence of the hero in reality, in every time period.

We predict them in our writings. The intelligence of the world of concept-heroes implies an apodictic intelligence that rules its possibility, the invisible spirit of its causes and performance. The dynamic of this possibility implies that it is one heaven in the universe, one rule, one source and one potential that is indicating the reality of these powers. The heaven of it all is the unique place which its assortment of possibilities from which the concept arrives, its place of reality in the heavens. It is the invisible aspect of surrounding auras and signs that understand the true dialectic of the hero and his life and times. The anticipation of him is his possibility, in dream and further duality/reality in the universe.

8.4 Blessings and Curses

In Concept-Art, the reality of life is the same, according to a person's fortune, and their blessings and curses, and what is equal in terms of equating standard. Concept-Art does not betray the prejudice of merit, and in all Concept-Art and imagination, the bitterness and the confidence of certainty of a person's fortune in life is met with the same acceptances that are in reality. In this way, one may be able to see why they may view their life as a concept-game, because the trans-disposition of a concept-game becomes equal to reality, and if the codes of fictitious hero's and stories are real, so that if all of the requirements of the story were met in real life, that in real life, that story would occur. Many fall below the power that is needed to use concept-art and gaming in order to make them an arcade that specializes in the capability that is required to meet this standard. I am devising that the Immortalae will use the arcades, especially that they generate, in order to train in reality. The Immortalae will beat the odds of the arcades, and they will specialize in fighting and concept-warfare.

Concept-Art is the realm of creation where perfected images represent the spirituality and the narration of examples which depict what would be necessary for Concept-Art to occur (an arcade). Specifically, there is a heightened power of opposing forces, and there is etiquette of life wisdom which gives the protagonist's a way of winning through physical tests, trials and combat and a way of not being hindered by the masses. The Event of the story must occur in the Immortalae's life, but he must have the proper settings and variables, such as the variables and settings of stories and concept-games. He must take them seriously (the games and characters and heroes), because they have it (the reality of opportunity), and he does not. If he does not regard them with intelligence, then he may not understand how to begin or fathom its occurrence. He has envied their way of life and their stories, and he has desired that his life would be a concept-game, that he could project and design what his life could be by imagining a concept-game [of power], but the emulation of the game is problematic, because he needs to be a hero before he can begin, and that is all he needs to be, so that he must accept the mentality that his heroism is more important than what is happening in society in order for him to accommodate the life of a concept-game, and many are not fit to participate. It does not matter what age he is. He must train and find his fight in the world. Immortalaeism supports this view of power and Concept-Art, that Concept-Art is an advertisement for reality that accommodates power because they are powerful, and it accommodates a storyline that displays how one becomes a hero after that persuasion, and that the arcade teaches how to beat fights in reality, the arcade is a school for heroes. He is always seeking heroism. He desires the adventure, and he desires the fight and the call of heroism, he is a hero. He will answer the call by relinquishing society and taking up his real life as a hero. He is blessed if his fight is a 'game' in Immortalaeism, and he is cursed if he does not possess the life of a hero, but he is one. He must understand their stories, and the wisdom of heroism, and how to accomplish heroism in the world. The Immortalae have envied all games and stories, and they have desired with an unquenchable thirst to be involved in the real fight, under the right preparation and fitness of life-circumstance. He must pursue it at all times, because it is the Spiritualism and the Religion of Immortalaeism, to partake in heroism. Immortalaeism is a Spiritualism (philosophy, spirituality, religion) that combines power, immortality, heroism and martial art/martial training into a complete way of life. By becoming Immortalae, he will be ready for heroism. How should he partake in the storyline of a concept-game – he must understand that the stories of the games are happening in the world, that they are real. The true hero has the pulse of wickedness, and he is always searching for an opportunity for heroism. The Immortalae is united to the cause of heroism, and every Immortalae will be a hero, and he will understand the secrets and the paths of heroism, and why it is so important. He will place Immortalaeism first, above all else, and he will be an Immortal-hero. He will give place to the cause of the hero, his own cause.

POWER III

The Immortalae will marry the Essence of Self
With the Essence of Power to unite themselves to Power
forever.

-Vaul Impera

1. Logic

Logic is antecedent to reality, it is in the construct. The incipience of logic is where power first meets differentiation. Before this even, power is in similitude, filling all of creation with an equanimity of power. Logic means 'other' in terms of its sequencing wisdom and its differentiation of modality which typify its interpretations. Truth is substantive to all logical claims, it is what matches as verified concerning existence, and logic is the force of compulsion that divides, because of the creational difference of difference itself. All claims are diminished in that all claims purport the same idea, so that they are diminished into one nota. Available claims are unique in that they are available from differentiated powers that are universal. These powers are arching potentiates that represent a belief and a cause, and the causes are perpetuated as potentiates in the ideal as powers themselves. Substantive claims decree a power in its difference. In existence itself, which is 'to be', there are arch-causes that proclaim the original difference in reality. Reason separates and is the verification of what is true, and because

1. Power is egalitarian
2. Truth is verification
3. Logic is the negotiation of truth
4. Reason then is nothing but an in impartial egalitarian negotiation of truths and knowledge.
5. Reality is the Truth of a Power, differentiated by Logic.

Logic then, because it knows that there is a difference in the inherent claim of existence, will separate the reality. The powers of creation divide once they emerge with the world, which is the incipience of logic, because at one time they converged in the same notions, until it was said "I do not think anything at all the same as what you think". Thus, an oracle of the world is devised of the division of theory from creations' categories, which is in *circumstance*, because of differentiation of inherent universal causes that insist on separation and negation. Thus, the way and the truth are said about existence according to its parameters. There is no other way in such circumstance than in identity, and non-identity means slavery because they must produce for someone else who possesses a greater identity in the original cause of creation. Thus, 'I am that I am'. Thus logic is the universal power of the intelligence of separation – SEGA, or else we would all be the same spirit, because we are different, we accept differentiation, that is, truth and logic. The clause above differentiation is 'for, against, neutral', and as a part of creation, we were once all 'one', until we said that I am nothing as the same as you are, and so we became different, and we see difference as reality, and this is the nature of reason, that by logic, we understand the 'isness' of all that is, its being-in-itself.

2. Reality

The reality is a thing that is beyond the super sensibility of the world. The reality forms in the understanding of powers movements, which grasp the manifold conditions of power. Such a reality that is its embodiment, so that power takes on a form, an epicentre, like liquid energy, the intelligence itself. Like a river, power fills whatever may take power, and so much power. Power surges on the energy of what is, it is sheer ability. There are no rules or regulations, no laws or edicts, there is only power. The reality is the way of power, and there is no other way. If it does not hold power, it does not make any sense to us. We inherently understand power and its balances. Power channels through the possibility of power, and it teaches its ways. Power is unrestrained potential, and it operates in dominion to sub-dominion, from principal to principal, behaviour to behaviour, league to league. For this, power exalts the highest domain, the most powerful, and provides unrestrained heights in the experience of power. Power is unrestrained potential. It is dangerous, it is circumspect to the entity which is a domain in itself, that occupies power. It is rapid, intellectual, wise, it always proves itself, it is accurate and magnanimous, it is precise but grand, manifold, replete of itself, concentrated potential, whole and undivided. Its dominion is first unhindered and uncontested, and second it makes itself perfectly expressed. All things have a source of power, and power is in everything. The boundary of power is what power denies, which restricts its potential. Power eternal is timelessness in respect of power, which is the source of power of things in general, it is the power that provides for the life and expanse of things, which is the energy that fills their domain. Power will not accept the words/commands and understandings against its more powerful dominion, and power gives them their place, it is the power of the races to express power in their individual manner, and that they should understand power in their own way. It is the harnessing of power that concentrates power, it is the method of power that the harnessing of human potential understands, not by understanding virtue or logic or the expressions of power, but by understanding power itself. In this, they must understand that in order to contain power, they must not deny the development of powers decrees, in its performance and understanding. They must avail themselves to the understanding of power itself, in order to become a student and an embodiment of great power.

Power denies all intellectualism that denies its domain, and all reason, or rhetoric. The expressions of power are separate and distinct, and some individuals access power through various expressions, and they are not as powerful in consideration or in reality with other powers, and they are of a sub-dominion. We take energy and mastery by understanding intellectualism, but we take greater exaltation by understanding power itself. To be powerful one must understand power at least, he must understand the limitlessness and the freedom of expressing great power, and that to be controlled and confined is a restriction of power. These are only variations of powers' prospect, but they do not change what the power is. The dialectic of how one understands in life is attributed to how one manages the power that they receive, and what type of power they have sourced by their understanding of power. The dialectic of how one manages their behaviour and their inner/apperceptive state, is the discussion of power, how they manage power, which determines how much power they can receive, which is human behaviour. The entire world is only an expression of power, and so is spirituality and religion and intellectualism. They are methods by which one receives and expresses power. Honesty is the way, integrity is the modus, and purity is the sourcing, of the fashioning of being that will understand how to express power. The entire world is only the expression of various powers, and the height of intellectual understanding, including spiritual, is only the method of winning the favor of power or of deciding on a fundamental truth. The human spirit is a container of a spiritual construct that needs virtue in order to succeed, it is a construct of humanities identity, and individual identity, and its relationship to the cosmos. Once virtue has met its full excellence, he will understand a transformation and an alignment of being that will result in a transcendent identity that does not doubt according to the lie and the character of will, and he will channel the full merit and unerring reality of his behaviour. He is ready to receive greater power upon the accomplishment of the fashion of virtue and its mark, excellence. The microcosm and the discussion and dialectic of intellectualism and its plurality is a very serious game of selecting and dividing power. The human spirit is a crystal that is finely cut. The diadem of intersecting light is the centre around which there is spirituality, religion and intellectualism and being itself, and belief, which help to create the identity of the gemstone. The expressions of the world are the expressions of the spiritualism, intellectualism, and religion that is present. Idolatry is following a thing itself, such as gold, in the application of the apprehension of the spirit. The totems of power, and their terms, are the understandings of the spirits and intellectualisms that are in the world. Out of the darkness comes the light of power itself. It is power that convinces us, and it is power that challenges. We draw power from sources of power, how much we seek power sometimes determines how much we understand that power, in regard to entitlement. We turn to power in our times, in order to draw the energy of that power from its concentration, sometimes the concentration is in the centre of a nation, in its most powerful people, they surround the power itself, and all customs and laws are made after the understanding of the power. Men are crowned with power. Those that hold the most power understand power, and they are possessed by the necessities of power. The reality of power is undeniable, to understand power will make her like a god in the earth, because all things have their existence, height and potency by power, and by power alone. In order to understand the world, one must only understand power.

3. Essence

Power is strong. Power is bold. Power is self-assured. Power is realistic. Power is pragmatic and practical. Power is itinerant. Power is certain. Power is disciplined. Power has one path. Power has one dialogue. Power is free and perfectly managed. Power understands everything that pertains to its existence. Power must accept lowering to a greater power, or else defiance. Power itself is confidence. Power is harmony of self. Power is proper identity. Power selects its own understanding, always. Every power has its own truth. Power dictates that there is a reason for everything that happens that accords with understanding. Greater powers order smaller powers that agree. Greater truths govern smaller truths. Truth and power are united in the expression of entity. What something 'is' is a truth, where a 'truth' is understood by essence and being itself, and power is the expression of what it is. Being will always express after its own understanding, and it will use power to do so. The purity of being may more fully express power than a corruption of being. Honesty will turn toward a power, integrity will understand it, and purity will draw it closer to the reality of the power. Courage is the depth of powers commitment. Strength is the severity of the energy of power. Love is the adoration of power. Temperance is discipline of power. Fearfulness is the knowledge of power. An increase in power is an increase in all virtues, and all ability. An increase in power breaks the limitations of power, and the limitations of understanding. An increase in power is an exaltation of being, because of magnanimity, understanding, and effectiveness. The inner essence of power is expressed in the corporeal, physical and actual form of an entity or being. The essence of power is in all things that pertain to the expression of a being or entity. The intelligence and power of a being or entity is in its function or purpose. Intellectual truth is scaffolding that is lateral, and power itself (perhaps principle) is scaffolding that is vertical. The principle of the worlds rule wavers between certainty and uncertainty. Since we do not understand what we are to become, we postulate power and theory, and explore the cosmos physically and intellectually, in order to understand the circumstance of humanity, and this is the current essence of humanities power in the world, totally. There are proclamations of rigidity of understanding, but most are elementary, and some require much faith and no evidence. Theology is the application and understanding of the command of the spirit of a deity. The escalation of theology is the understanding of the cosmos after the limitlessness of moral law, his knowledge, and it is the limit of his presence and power who possesses truth in the cosmos. In this, the essence of reason and rectitude has brought moral visibility into the world, and the essence of worship of any deity is to conform and possess after its power. The power of the deity is coveted because of power by imagination or spiritual knowledge, and also because of identification. The theology of deities and the worship of them is the escalation of being into the conformity of that power itself. The identity of power is that the purity and the connection of being has found a source of unending power, and that it has permitted his entity to unite with its entity, and he must not betray his source of power. In this, the gods were worshipped for their sources of power, for the strength of absolution. It is also what is correct/proper/right, because of identification. Eternal life is the essence that one should make the power of their being unending, and the expression of what that power is would manifest in the being. Eternal power is power that is unending, and considers only the unending, thus, I have proven that the argumentations of Immortalaeism are correct. Belief is that natus, the navigation and trajectory or direction of being and entity, and it is by choice that that entity should become, and it is by the fashioning of will and representation of spirit (intellect, spiritualism and religion) that he should find his way to power, and it is possible that he should be born with power at his command. Imperiosos and imperium is the understanding of command, and it is the essence of power that it understands its own certainty, and so it understands its own command and response to things in general. Eternal command is the command of life, of mortal life, and this is the essence of unending power, it is the everlasting in men that has taken the general respect of 'immortal', and it is the command of life that is considered wisdom in the world, and it is unending power that is the coveted command of empires, and eternal command of life is all of these things, and the essence of eternal life is the correction from mortality, which is to identify and connect with the eternal source of power itself. To overcome death is the greatest achievement of self, because in it are the works of unending power, and the identity and knowledge of self becomes the greatest achievement, because it is the knowledge of self without death that is the identity that is consumed in itself in unending satisfaction, and from a immortal nativity is brought immortality, and the immortal is born in that understanding eternal life was to understand how not to die, and to understand immortality is to be born into the immutable self, which is not the life that cannot die, eternal, but the self that cannot die or change, immortal. Achievement is often linked to death because it means expression of identity and the successfulness of self. The peace of immortality over achievement is that his achievement come from a self that will not change. This is the essence of power, that power will express after the identity of its spirit. The spirit of power itself and the essence of which Immortalaeism considers is the unending power, which is borne through eternal and immortal fire. It is the object that the Immortalae understand that they must consume their beliefs through fire, and they must create eternal fire, and then immortal fire, and bringing eternal and immortal power to their beings, they alleviate themselves from death. It is the identity and the connection of powers, that fire is a medium of purification that through which he may find the unending sources of power, that from, the fire refines and it will not be reduced to dust, ash and clay. The essence of unending power is that he would learn from unending power, how to be eternal, and how to be powerful. In this fire that is eternal or immortal, he will place in his mortality, and it will be reduced to ashes. But when he places that which is eternal or immortal into the fire, the elements remain. As in mortal spiritual fire, the elements remain.

In the universe, we must express greater power, greater words (which are commands), and propensities (action). To incline to power is first, to act upon power is second, and to reach a higher power is to take the inclination, and a harness of perfect actions, and through understanding and learning about higher power, and also how to be a medium that communicates power effectively, that he begins to replace the complexities of his dominion with new understandings, and reaches a taste of new power. In this, his position has not changed, but he is capable of reaching higher power, when his alignment and purity agree with greater power. The channel of power is so deep and powerful, raging with the elemental enactments of power and display, it is only that he would accept the surge, understand the teachings of power, and allow power to flow through his life. The power available is kept away by the ruminating of the mind, where belief may break-down and rebuild in the mind, but the process comes upon the projectile of belief. It must be broken to power in order to accept the rule of power, because it understands various things that are circumstantial, but it does not comprehend that it is only in a shallow experience of power, and that a great current and storm of power is being avoided. To be a part of what power does, we receive from power, and we are on the shores of power, but in order to experience more power, we need to allow for greater power, to incline and open our vision to power, and see it and its governance in the fabric of the world and cosmos, and to draw into power by allowing greater power to influence belief. This means that there is more power available with which to live, and that by orienting his life to power, that he is awakened past the comforting expression of identity, to universal and worldly cosmological energy, that is, he begins to understand universal intelligence and accept greater power. He must accept power before he accepts belief, or he does not know of what rank he will be. He will only see his belief if he places it first, what the Immortalae must see is a combination of power, eternal life/immortality, with understanding. The paradigm of intellect has less significance. The Immortalae needs to know power and immortality, or he knows nothing at all.

4. Consciousness

Consciousness becomes the real fruit and food, the primary source of nourishment. Whether through meditation, spiritual practices or matters of circumstance and experience, consciousness is that altus, the altitude of thought and understanding. By generating more powerful thoughts and realities, he may play with his energy, and he may break down rudimentary belief systems, and develop furtherance in understanding. Consciousness is literally the awareness and the intelligence of the entity or being, and it is also the projections from the being, such as projects, constructions and inventions, all of which come from the development of consciousness, and are stolen in the markets of the world. Self-awareness is consciousness, and universal awareness is consciousness. Consciousness means that I am aware of whatever is transpiring, and it means thought-generation. To raise the level of consciousness, he must realize a greater reality, which means that his understanding of reality will graduate, but that he will not forsake inherent truth. This can be done through meditation, and he must meditate and become aware of the object of his meditation, in order to understand it. Everything he already understands is within his grasp of reality. Meditation at times is to pierce with the intuition and the intellect and the being, to sense a greater moment, or awareness. Knowing is an object of meditation, and knowing is consciousness. Consciousness is involved with the mind, and the spirit of the being. Consciousness, meditation and awareness are conceived by the being, the spirit of the being is an electric cloud, and the electricity is the will, and the vibrancy of the electricity is consciousness, and consciousness is the reality and the connection to the source of the power of the being, and the cloud, or sensible energy, is the projected energy of the being, which is the sensibility of the spirit, and the identity of the being is united with the will, which is the generator of belief. It is belief that can bring insensibility to us, so that we cannot see or hear, so we must produce consciousness by meditation because it brings the sensibility to our spirit to understand, and we must understand power. Power is not divided, it is integer, it is one and whole, and power is the remedy for spiritual blindness, and it is what we are trying to understand, because it brings a greater reality. Greater power is above, and it is in-front, so that we must incline to its essence. Consciousness is spiritual energy that brings vibrancy and heightened understanding, and greater spiritual power, and greater reaction/awareness to the world, and we must look to power to obtain it. Power is high, and in order to approach power, the world believes that they must be pure, and they argue and fight, because power is not approached in the proper regard. And the highness of power creates the orders of civilization, and they pay the proper respects, because they want to acknowledge power in the proper fashion. They are fearful for power, and from it they derive temperance and duty. They covet power, and to be first before power, and chosen. They create elitisms, and conceal power, because many do not understand. It is the order of power in men that creates such behaviours, in what they understand about powers orders. Power is above, and in-front, except they may need to venture backward and face forward, in order to properly stand before power, in the case of mistakes and falls – this means that they have already fallen, and the power they once held is above them and in front of them again. When a power is excelled, it is mastered, it becomes childlike, and greater power becomes available. In many things, we show our mistakes by bowing our heads, and we show our fearlessness by showing our faces. We cannot face the face of our uncertainty, but we are confident to face the face of our confidence. We would die to face uncertainty. We will live again if we face certainty, which is pragmatism, which is the fruit of perseverance.

In idolatry and religion, the face of power has been in the sun and in the moon and the stars, and lower powers but still great, have been in the earth. It is nothing but proverbial that man's circumstance with power is evident in the cosmos, and that the constancy of the heavens has been aligned with the everlasting. His mastery of the seas, and dominance of the land, is as the propensity of his power, his rule over them does not experience identity with them, as recited of a god, but his dominion is the earth, and in inclination of the sun and its identity and the moon and its identity and the stars and their identity will rule in power, and they will be inclined to for understanding. He understands the faculty of power, the systems of intelligence and order, but he does not understand a more powerful order that he can imagine, but has never seen. This is considering the limitations of man's power, and the identity of man as a being, and what his power is.

In empires, the power to rule the earth is in power itself, and that power has belonged to various forms. From man to man, the greatest power in the earth is immortality. It is the consciousness of power that leads to a source of power. He must use the powers of nature and the seas and the storm to understand how he must come out from his shelter and comfort and lose his life to understand power. Concealed in the world, for man, is power immeasurable.

Out of the progression of the human spirit come new idea, revelations, inventions, new understandings, adaptations, revisions and projects, and it is the projection of consciousness, and the construction of ideas and progress that generate more power, and furtherance in the aptitudes, through meditation. Meditation becomes the vocation, and the art. He must understand that we make and break consciousness together, and form generations through consciousness, and we deviate through meditation, and it is only through the connections of the mind, in which we say that we have made our fifty privates in the military are equal to fifty of the opposition's captains. It is power that does this, because by understanding power he understands a greater reality, and a greater essence, and a greater consciousness of understanding.

Consciousness then, is awakening to greater awareness through power and meditation. Without witnessing it in his consciousness, how should he apprehend to believe? Thus, the portal to greater power is in the construct of meditation, in the way that he perceives life/power. A greater reality awaits him in the witness of meditative practice. He must cast down society's frame of mind and in meditation he must seeks the answers that he needs by seeing without the worlds influence.

5. Baptism

He must lose his life for power. He must accept that immortality is the greatest power to a man, because it is that men die at the boundary of death behind them, and immortality before them. Those that use death as a power, have chased men, killing them with deaths power. The cycle of death and its occurrence is the wisdom and the conversation of man, it is the undertone and the overtone of much exploit and civilization, and it is only those who have grappled and dealt with death and life-everlasting that are free from it. Death, the greatest problem in the earth, the greatest part of the conversation of man, the lesson of death and its involvements is merely error says power, it is only that he has denied the entire problem of death that he understands how to accept death, because he has not chosen it. How then should he think immortality? But he already knows that the problem of death is in spiritual disease from the world, and that the remedies bring life everlasting. Thus, the problem of immortality is the problem of death, according to many. So then, immortality is related to death, as much as belief, with belief I can believe in one or the other, and I can believe in both, but not both ultimately, which means that to believe in both falls out. Much of the conversation of man and of slaves is death, and the error of their way is corrected by statute, and it bends the back of men under the weight of its understanding, but in the face of the accomplishment of its truth is to stare into the face of the sun, because it has beaten death and witnessed immortality. The laws of religion have lowered men because they are struck by them as much as they *will*, and it is in the balance of immortality that he weighs his life, because all else is nothing. He must consume his life in unending power, and feed his life into the flames of eternal life and immortality, and he will understand the correction of power, where unending power is power that will never fail, a power that he must connect with and make it the source of his life's power. Power has been sought arduously, and it has become the centre of the edifice of power, and it has filled many with its way. To identify with a race is to identify with a source of power. To compliment a sect is to compliment their source of power. Many sources of power, and ways or organizing belief of various heavenly or earthly constants have been found, and they have various effects and outcomes. Power orders their behaviour, their traits, it selects them all together and raises the edifice, it understands their speech and their intelligence, it is revered and feared, and worshipped, it is their respects, it is their sense of successfulness, because they need to know it in order to identify with what they believe, and with what is adopted as identical with what they understand for protection, for sufficiency, for worth, these are all the reasons for selecting power. We all have a source of power, and a place where we venture in order to meet that power, and that is the power that we have in order to understand life, it is the power that we use for the things that we need in life, and we need the baptism of Immortalaeism, in that I have described that our sources of power should be unending power, and that he should incline to understand greater power, in order to understand power, and to understand its propensity, its magnanimity, its supremacy, and its imperium. Power will destroy, its eminence will wear upon that which is not really power, it will break under the force of power and bow to it. A greater power will be so fearful that it will shape the construct of society, it will bring humility to the spirit, in case of offense. It will shape helmets, weapons, speech, reverence, intelligence, rule, governance, societal structure, and it will shape all of it so that it knows powers uniformity. Money systems, business, religion, nationality, all of these things could change, if power increased, or if power decided to change or modify. Nothing would exactly be the same, only a memory of what was intelligent, after immeasurable power has been received. To think and consider is to think with power, or not at all. It is not the invention or the plan that we seek, it is greater power. The universal understanding, the surge and powers of the cosmos are only truly understood through power. To increase power is to increase experience, it is not the foolishness of many ideas and adaptations and plans, the fossils of the generations of the mind, it is undeniable power, the purity of power and the cosmos. It is the alignment with power, the agreement that allows it to be understood, and to be identified with.

6. Substance

The relationship of things, of anything, is how it relates by power, for all things are under the dominion of power, and it is by power that we understand, and by nothing else. To be close to the substance of power may mean that he is close to the rule of things. Power is first spiritual, before it is manifested in actuality or physicality. The dominion of power is governed with law and principle, it is the consciousness of the reality of the world that determines how much we understand of power, we can plan things, but it is better to be more powerful. Power will fill all things that are connected together, and it will run it until the end. The substance of power is pure energy, without corruption or defect or deformity. He must return to the substance of power constantly, in order to fully understand its power, to absorb its power and eminence. Upon understanding where one's power is, he must face it constantly in order to understand the meaning of power, and to understand the intelligence of power. However, power will occupy whatever belief system he has, and it will fulfill it until the end, in the reality of the world, even if it means death. Judgement accommodates the mental time of the multitudes, according to their structures of power, because they do not understand the mind of power, and the eternal and immortal mind. This is the demoniac mind, that is based in fear. Virtue vaguely teaches the opposite of a fearful mind, because the truth of virtue is not moved by the world, or by a demonic influence. The immortal does not change, he does not seek to control, and he is not led astray by temptation (in this he has the power over the mind of the demoniac). The immortal would never fight with the insanity of a fearful mind, as a demon. He needs to become that which produces what he needs, but it is not his needs that he understands, he must understand the self. He understands that without the protection of virtue or eternity in the mind, the patterns of the spiritually dead mind are constant in seeking a hierarchy of demonic structure. It is that we observe them, that their minds are of a different nature. They are patterns that are bent on wicked gratification and service. They are always calculating appearances and determining their position by estimating what the power of temptation is. It is an edifice of judgements that are ruled ultimately by the knowledge and power of temptation. This mind can be exchanged for the quiet and peaceful mind of presence that fills the mind and body by becoming aware of one's surroundings, and quieting the mind so that it does not perform wicked impulses, it is the timeless mind. In this mind, away from the world, in meditation, there is no personality of name or form, or writings or history, and there is nothing influencing outside, with this meditative insight, meditation becomes profitable, because one can pierce with insight into negotiations and obtain clarity. This is spiritual eternal light, illuminating within. It is a gift that comes by leaving evil worldly concourse, purging it and purifying himself, using the light to find awareness in life, to find the path without evil. He has decided that they are patterned, wicked, he desires the inner light. The light is now within him so that he may find his way. Now he is not distracted by them, or influenced, or without thought, becoming one of them – now he may begin. A light that is beyond time is now guiding him, an eternal light that shines over the truth of the temporal world (discernment). Now he has the four quarters of his being guarded, now he can see across land and territory and persevere against evil. A mind guided by the eternal light will fill the body and purge him from evil within, and heal him. Without being placed in position by worldly concourse, he can find his eternal place in the world, the Eternal is a portal to a manifestation of his beginning and eternal purpose in the world. While he is in the eternal domain, he is immune to many evil attacks on the mind. His light of perception will now pierce the darkness, and he will see further territories in the world, and wisdom will avail itself to him. His confidence will increase in spiritual force, his intimidation and power of effectiveness. The unregenerated mind cannot find the eternal light, because it cannot cease from planning and judging after patterns and hierarchies of wickedness to no avail, it cannot find the eternal in meditation, because its spirit cannot commit to the timeless and formless beyond the world that is eternal, the spirit must align with eternal requirement, but it must cease from seeing wickedness and the hierarchies of damnation. That is what the spirit views to comprehend before physical visibility, it means that whether they admit it, they have given themselves over and are working for a wicked kingdom or domain in the world. The timeless eternal may be found by passing the business of the world, without name or form, without labels from the world or its attachments. Attachments to the world will pull from the world, and consume the mind in needless mental activity. This activity is meant to pull him into the world, as bait, and line him up in the worlds business. The patterns of the mind comprise the self, as demonic (whether known or not), and its involvement in the organization of the world. The light of the eternal is beyond time, and independent from the world. The eternal is beyond mortality, and death is a great obstacle to the timeless eternal dimensional. These are the teachings of what is commonly called 'no-mind' meditation, but in Immortalae is called, the art of the meditative 'Dragon', and the Immortalae must possess this meditation at all times, and be filled with its energy and power.

By filling with power, we understand all that we may understand of power, and then we must demonstrate the quality of that power, by wisdom and action. This is growth, and this is maturity, that we seek power to understand it, and once proven, we return to the source of power to understand more of it. When we deny power, we invite death. At times, we reject because we require more understanding, and special care, it is this retreat that allows power to understand the point at which there is upset, to receive the correction of understandable woes is simply great victory in those areas.

Power is instant, it understands all of the emotions of the spirit, and interprets them perfectly. A power source cannot be lied to, not power itself. The true modus of the spirit is what is understood by power, it takes the full integer into its balances, and cannot be defrauded of the true intent of seeking its purpose. In this, we create our own experience with power, with the cosmos, and it is the true commands and identity of the spirit that bring experience. Power that cannot be lied to is and will tell all that it understands is honestus, it is for those that are honest. It is for those that are mature that can accept lies from power, because they understand that by the acceptance of what their spirit maintains, is what they will receive, and there is no plea for honesty, they will either know or not know, based on what they themselves understand. In this regard, it makes sense that the races drew upon different powers, and for that reason, they accepted different symbols of power, and different gods, and different characteristics. It is because of power, and what is accepted by *his* power, that there are differences by power. It is by power that there is reason, and by power there is governance of dominion. Power is in every seat of world dominion, and they can only become what they understand of power. The boundary is power, and the most powerful sometimes stretch the farthest boundary, or they may place the most power at the boundary that they possess. The communication of power is the negotiation of boundary, of territory, and of governance. Power determines these things, in every aspect of dominion, power determines what it is. The creation of new paths of understanding, are empirical in the world, and the expression of greater power has an expression in regard to dominion in the world, which begins with the understanding of power that is within the entity, and how they decide that they understand power, reflects in the world according to boundary and territory.

7. Forma

The power of form has many shapes, and in the end, all things take the form of their power, but not all forms are exemplary, they are deformed and show corruption and unintelligence, but power fulfills the intelligence of that which it inhabits. Power is the essence behind form, and power is its method of being. Power is the method, but intelligent design is the artifice. The power of a wall is no longer powerful if it does not fulfill its purpose. It is also the purpose for which power is suited which dictates whether or not a thing is powerful. The purpose is the reason of power, and it is responsible for the expression of power. It is only through the communication of power that there is understanding, and only through the truth of power that there is possibility, or mutability or inevitability.

The form of power in men is intersecting lines of understanding that form dominion and governance. Every man forms dominion, and in respect of this, I understand a metaphor of stones that shine light within them, gems. In this respect, they are the heart of the spirit, the identity, and the will, they are the essence and the generation of where power comes from, and what it appears as. The very essence of something is the centre of its being, the centre of its substance and entity, and where the generation for all of its effect is derived. To simply describe power is to describe the dominion of all things, it is to understand the power that is behind all dominion, which is the understanding of unending power, and that which supplies all temporal power, and it is the agreement with unending virtues and alignments that I have described that will bring greater power. Power beyond what we know is power that has not been accessed, and it has not been manifested in the spirit. It would likely destroy our intelligent systems of belief, and shatter our values, such as immortality. The form of power is within man, in order to perform powerful works, he must understand power, the power of his skill with power, and the manner in which he interacts with power, which is also his vocation. All known beings interact with power, and it is the wisdom of men to understand how, and by what manner and intelligence that they perform their works. Differing wisdoms, and differing types of power. The form of the power is visible, it is present, it is before, because the expression of the essence of power brings the effect, and the effect is its spirituality, or its physicality. The form is after the intelligence of power. In this regard, it is the principle of the being that brings its form, and the lines of accepted belief, which are actually mandates and commands creating dominion, that generate his outer influence, and the constitution of his being. It is his relationship to the cosmos. its birth from the metaphysics of its creation. In the field of belief, belief is before action, which is the command of a man or an entity. It is the metaphysical manifestation of relation to him in which he is not content with, with his life. He wishes to increase, to gain. The philosophers remedy to his poverty then, is to move lines metaphysically by selecting a new doctrine, by becoming and being redefined in the metaphysics, in his veritas. These lines move naturally as men age, and they also move by his intelligence, belief and spirituality. This is how doors open, and doors close, this is how he becomes not only chosen, but approved and rested in his own accomplishment of masculine being. Immortality is the change of self into immutability, it is the rejection of the world and its temporal spirits and spirits of death and its intellectualism, replaced by power itself. He must tear down the house of his intellect which he has built as a man, and he must select power. He must tear down his entire house for his being, and only select that which may last forever, including personality. He has filled his house with mediocrity and partial theories, he has sought it all in the world. This is over in Immortlaeism, we only select power and immortality (virtue proper understanding) and the sword/martial arts (meditation guardianship), there is nothing else.

8. In Demonstration

The reality that is posed with higher unifying concepts is that there is a synthesis of powers, in the reality of what is common between them. In this, we begin to understand how to venture beyond the concept of duality. We wish to fold these powers and experience another dimension of reality. We wish to finish these realms of limited possibility, and climb the ladder of the universe. In Immortalaeism, I proposed that the accomplishment of a side of duality, was to fully understand a field of power from the orb of its knowledge, in truth. In order to select through the orbs of power, we must navigate accomplishment, which I have extolled already. Being powers in themselves as orbs and dualities, we must understand their power, and we must master the power in-itself. Because they are opposites, there is a trigger in the higher unifying concept that divides the behaviours, and dictates that the performance of one, is to decline in the progress of the other. This is a stipulation of creation in the metaphysics. This implies that for every possible choice, there are at least two paths. In this, in finding one's way through the spheres of duality, we do not have one choice, but always two, in order to make a choice between them. In this, is fatalism and destiny. We must accomplish the spheres of creation in dualism, and we shall be finished our selecting, and we will meet the end of what creation has to offer. Things such as male and female, we have only one choice, and it cannot be changed, we must accept the full sphere of being male, or the full sphere of being female. We understand then, a position in creation, that to accept the full responsibility of possibilities in dualism, that we arrive at the fullness of the possibility of our being. So the orbs that contain and separate power are the possibility of what he may become. I will stipulate that the imputations of intelligence and being itself in the universal creation of voluntary will in regard to people is that of a processional nature, since the indication intuitively is obviously that we assume higher understandings by graduating through the question of understanding. The 'orbs' of power are limited and they can be counted in what pertains to the frame of our existence. As masters, he must understand how to accomplish two before he reaches the dimension of three (orbs, tripartite spirits and domains). Creation becomes a park, and success becomes a perfecting and a perk of being, to be a master and the embodiment of godly knowledge, greater than the edifice of man, is the being himself, all of them, not outclassed by the accumulation of civilization. He must sift the orbs of power and find the essence of his power, in order to have the highest ability in the world. The orbs of power and the spirits of Toxycant, illuminate the spiritual architecture and the mastery of creations apostolic theory and game for Immortalae, that due to the inherent organization of power and the law tables of its existence, that from infancy to the height of possibility of power (perfection), by his selection is his power determined, and in which capacity. Power is now sufficiently understood in its inherent place in the cosmos in Immortalaeism for the Immortalae.

NOT ALL ARE CHOSEN.
IMMORTALAEISM.

HERO

"I found him, he is here… the symbol of our virtue. What is his name?"

    -Vaul Impera

…immortality…the manifestation of a pure, life-giving essence/spirit.

    -Vaul Impera

Hero

Hero in Immortalaeism means '*Immortal-Essence*'.

The world has accepted that I am not a part of its business. The business of the Immortalae is that he focuses on development, and he will understand more than institution because it does not understand who he is. He is a ninja, because he will not understand what society does, because he will not understand their governance. I was asked if I was a superhero, I responded and said "No", and the man took me for a police officer off duty. He told me to be careful, as he communicated that the area that I was approaching downtown was very dangerous, and he warned me of the problem. Over the past few years I have been called many things, and perceived in many ways, being asked if I am a god. I realized in respect of this, that in what I was doing at that time, I had drawn attention to myself, from the cultivations that I was working toward in my private life, that in pursuing purposes of ascendance and martial arts, elitism and heroism and the virtues including justice, and realizing that I was very different because I did not understand society in what I was accomplishing. People in my city were also becoming aware of the difference of my accomplishment, which I discovered was emanating from me in the streets of society, and they understood that my actions were showing that I was more intelligent, and they understood me as powerful, a sign of progress. This is a manuscript to reveal the nature of the hero, which involves superheroes and concept-heroes and tales and stories, in relation to immortality, which is in order to illustrate to the Immortalae. This is also similarly the story of the ninja as a hero, because he does not use society for guidance, and he does not understand their rule, because they do not know him. The ninja will not appear before society as guilty, and neither will the hero. Society's corruption is the business of the ninja, and also of the hero.

I have courted the archangel, Lucifer, for a season and a few years, as I am familiar with him, who asked me if I would take two kingdoms from him, and later he offered me a part over the world. I have also entertained the Greek gods, in that Zeus asked me to be as a son to him, and to begin he asked me to be a Spartan. I was also approached by Odin, who has offered me a place with him in the afterlife. I have also been told that I will become a god, and I have been transfigured into a god but refused it. I was approached by and given the promise of Power itself, and I was selected for knighthood into the procession of the holy grail, and am familiar with the gods of the Zodiac. I have discovered Eternal Life and Immortality by my spiritual elitism, in which I found immortality immediately when I searched for it, which contributed to the promise of writing this book, Immortalaeism, a Spiritualism, which I began in concept when I was eight-teen.

When I was eight-teen I was shifted from a deep intellectual life, to a deep spiritual life. I had an eternal epiphany (enlightenment) at a high school graduation party. I was exalted over the party in the spirit, and I saw the event from a higher plane of existence. The Buddha would say I was awakened, and a chord of *destiny* snapped as my life flashed before my eyes, and I saw the destiny of *my truth*, as I saw the people at the party as if we were playing a cosmic game of chess, and with higher understandings, I stepped over their game, and I predicted all of their intelligences and dominions as if they were too simple, and predictable. Astrologically, I went to the end of the party astra-positionally and I knew that in my understanding that I was no longer using society to understand the circumstance. I ran into the most desired girl at the party alone in the main entrance, and I looked at her from a higher plane, and as a result a fight broke out over her and I, and thirty people started fighting and shouting in the kitchen. I went outside and stared at a full moon on a grass field in the country in delirium, and my friends stood around me in a semi-circle, and we had to leave as a result. The next day I prophesied, drawing company and friends, for about six hours and there was a permanent cosmic shift in my consciousness. I now understood fundamental spirituality, and I had an epiphany of writing a world religion. I could see the unconscious desires of people, I could see a deeper truth and reality behind the circumstance. It was at this point when I was taken above the world and shown where a war between Good and Evil would begin. I was shown these things in astral projection. When I was given the spirit of prophecy, I saw that I would be the author of a universal spirituality, my own spirituality which I saw in the epiphany. In these events, I was called to be a spiritual master and military leader in spiritual war. Before I knew world history, I saw in a prophetic vision where this war would begin, and I was called and asked what position I would take in regard to the war. I envisioned Immortalaeism at eight-teen years old.

Heroism, it is becoming a champion and a guardian. In youth, he will find what is valuable to him, and he may have a problem in understanding how he must stand before the people. He must accept the burden of his problem, and accept its challenges. He must align himself with the problem of his sympathies and personal world view. He must resolve a discipline where he may abdicate his own desires in self governance, and be fashioned as a robust, disciplined, masculine, cultured, discreet, prudent, and accomplished person. In youth, he must resolve the problems of his own life, and the society that he is in. He must be given to intellectualism and spiritualism. He must relinquish luxury and sensuality, he must be frugal, and the worth of his person will be a life that does not concede to temptation. He must shun wealth and riches in material form, and afford spiritual and intellectual wealth. He will learn that what is valuable to him is worth affording if he understands its value in his trade as a hero and warrior/fighter. He will understand the concourse of the world. For the immortal-hero, the greater cause becomes the power of his excellence and of his will, and further, it becomes perhaps a part of his character and persona. At times, the resilience of the hero lies within his ability to believe in his cause, and that he must find great purpose in what he does in the world. He must be glad to compromise a domesticated life with struggle, problem, danger and difficulty in exchange. He welcomes the threat of a great adversary, admires the fight, covets the opportunity to convey his meaning. In order to represent the problem, he must instill his belief, and they are a sign of his fight, and the sign that he makes as a hero. He must embody an equal truth and resolution that is as powerful as the lie and the problem in the world. He must know that he will be a hero, and that he will be the one that understands what he needs. He will not understand anything else except that he is a hero.

A hero is a leader. He will understand that he is a leader because he will make a powerful sign before the people, and it does not mean that he holds audience or that they must follow him and mind him. He will be the leader because he understands how to bring down an adversary. Being self-ruled and governed, he will produce a challenge that is capable of contra with great opponents in combat and in intellectualism and spiritualism, he will develop great personal power.

He will shatter the idiocy of public mind and foolishness as he rises to power, as he has a high regard for the high statures of people. He must leave the regular participation in society and of domesticated life, and in the prowess of his wisdom, he must look to find the heroic virtues that concern his universal problem, and the consciousness of a hero will begin to be born within him. As he begins to find his real values, he becomes the pristine, unique, fashioned image of a hero. His preferences, his meditations and his manner and personality will produce a different kind of hero. It is the travel of his soul, and where it ventures in contemplation that provides a distinct, solid formation of character. The intelligence of the hero is then expressed as the foundation of Immortal character, that has digressed from the common understandings of virtue and intelligence that are afforded in society. The hero finds a way to accept death, and he becomes ready to face his challenge. He has accepted himself in the view of immortality, and his challenge becomes the difficulty that he is prepared to surrender to its full occupation. He must find his Eternal Self, in pure consciousness without defilement.

A hero will prevail, either in life, or in death. He must not compromise his values through temptation or sedition, or evil concourse. A hero must continually accept the trials of virtue, and in the power of virtue, to find the wisdom that he needs, and the power to face a great adversary. Part of the wisdom of heroism is how the powerful principles that the hero uses to substantiate his being are used to manipulate what life offers into a unique wisdom, and the expression of a very powerful person, and what he allows to himself.

The hero may take the circumstance of a standard and a sign to the people, as a prophet is known to do. He is the consciousness of man without death, he is the essence of an eternal presence as Immortalae. He is the Eternal Virtue embodied, beyond time and death.

The hero will understand how to rule a home, society, a city, a nation, and he will understand how to fight, and he will understand power and war. In this, the virtue of masculinity, for a male, is indispensable. He understands the conformity of all governances, and he understands civilization. He understands the criminal, societal and international justice, and often his affairs take him to the notions that are not affected by the governance of law, to the lawlessness of offenses that threaten but are not caught by law. He finds himself grappling with evil and difficulties, and in the end, he must bear his belief as a shield and a symbol. He must learn to use his own scales [wisdom] and he will understand when he is called, as he understands the problem, and its cost to the people, and its wickedness. A hero is adept at finding wickedness more than most, and he understands it is his problem and not the problem of anyone else. He finds it because of where he is inclined to be, because he faces it in his spirit, he meets it in the places where he and his adversaries have a common understanding and taste for that which is dangerous.

Fidelity

Autonomy

In the nature of the Immortalae, he must persevere in order to convey trust, he must commit to his path at becoming eternal and immortal. In this, he must select a path of destiny that is aligned with the way he views himself in front of the human race because he is eternal. He will emerge at the end, at death, and he will be responsible for what he has chosen in life. In this, I mention a beginning of the unending in his will, from which he will not detract in his decision. In this, he considers his will, and he changes his fate. In creation there were many orbs among all of the terrain that belonged to man. An 'Orb' is a tree of knowledge, and its power. To access an orb of knowledge required knowledge and responsibility. In Immortalaeism, I teach that to select a fate, he must gather all of his orbs under one origin, and select that from that time, he will consider all things in life as he has chosen in all of his dualities. In this, he is sealing his fate, and he is choosing what his time in the world and beyond will be. He is beginning to select immortally. He cannot perform the actions that are not within the truth of his being, so that he cannot select falsely, without committing a lie, and losing his origin. Evil contains the same practicum as the good. Evil requires the same for survival, and the logic of all things is the same. For every action, there is both good and evil.

Transformations come with the realization of self, after the truth of self. In the knowledge of self, new truth causes him to realize further his identity, which cannot be changed or altered. Transformations are responsible for the way that he views himself, which is responsible for the office and the detail, and the way of his life. In fantasy, is the super-ego, he will understand how to accept the processional understandings between the realities, but he must accept new truth of his being, and incorporate it into his willpower. Transformations are also victories, they are progressions. They lead to callings and elections into higher rank and office in life. They come with license and verify stature.

The sign of mortality is subordination because it is wanted from him, and also the sign of death. The end of covetousness is slavery. It is slavery and covetousness and fear and utopia that is the subject of mortal intellectualism. The divine sin caused only slavery amidst the human race, the race fell when the temptation to secure false possession, and rule, spread through the people, and their temporary claims were made for pleasure and satisfaction, and they became evil.

Immortality

Part I

Exiter and Finality and Heroism

On a number of occasions I have received moments of eternal epiphany, where I view the world without illusionment, and I see it through the understanding of the Eternal Constant, which is the view from Eternal Life (of the energy source of virtue and power); now in martial arts, this is my perpetual view, to understand the essence of martial arts, and my own essence eternally. What else could Exiter or Finality, Eternal or Immortal life imply except the experience of it? To understand Eternal Life is to be conscious of the Eternal, and to be filled with the Eternal Being, and Immortal life is the realization of immortal consciousness, but also possession of the life as well, and crossing from mortality, to eternity, and to immortality. The Immortalae must understand the realization of Eternity within his being, and also of Immortality. As eternal and immortal he must trust that his being will never change, and that his presence eternal will push out the worldly image of himself (false representation of self), and the timeless eternal self will pervade in his mind and spirit, and he will no longer need to strain to see the truth of the world in front of him, when he can see it through the view of the eternal. He needs to unidentify with his entire mind and understand that his way of life as a mortal is in the way of Evil, in mind, body, spirit and feeling. The world has offered a catalogue of sinfulness to divide his time daily, of identity and appetite, to select which false self he will prevail in in the world. In Immortalaeism he relinquishes his identity in the world, and he apprehends his true nature without the influence of dead forms, or eternal evil. He must find his eternal self outside of the worlds time. In eternity, he cannot desire that his life should change from his eternal place. In Immortality, he does not desire that his understanding of self should ever change unless it is to know more about who he 'is'. In the eternal, he cannot understand what it is without understanding what life is (the value of innocence, the divorcement of life from death).

The world will become simple to the Eternal and the Immortal. They will begin to see what is theirs in the world, after they have been cured from the blindness of mortality and covetousness, and have extinguished the desires of ever wanting what belongs to someone else and that of evil, they will begin to become immortal. They will master the trivial circumstance of doubting, mortal men and temporalism and its understandings, and the idiom of ridding of the *final evil* against oneself. They will find that the experience of mortals is mostly the subject of death and dead forms, and forms that are dying spiritually; but that the destiny and providence of mortality illuminates the purpose and decency of their humanity. It becomes obvious that these spiritual ideas are within, and they understand more because they understand more about the illumination of the being, that the spirit gives rise to its belief, and it manifests them and extols them and permeates them through its being, into its dominion. To make immortal choices is a sign that one is able to understand eternal light and providence and also formlessness, the world unmanifested, beyond subject or object or name or form or history. You must ignite the flame of Eternal and Immortal life, and feed it your desire so that they are scorched by the destructive flames of the Immortal and Eternal, so that all that remains is the beginning elements that are useful as Immortalae, just a man with nothing in life except an eternal or immortal life. He must end externicism before becoming Immortalae, that is, he must end the worship of dead forms and dead spirit. The mortal has a dead personality through the veneration of dead spirits so that his life is in replication of them. His desires will become Eternal and Immortal, and he will begin to extend his life throughout all of time, knowing that he must search for immutability, his immutability, and his life as Immortalae will become evident. The end of all things begins with the end of mortality. The end of death is the end of mortal life. He must accept that he must not attempt to control life and he must seek permanence through acceptance of circumstance, and not through its manipulation. The unregeneration of self (mortal death), is found in his problems in that his want and his unwant are the same desire of false personality that arise through his identification with dead external forms. He must seek non-control (permanence) and to walk away from alluring things (no desire), so that he is no longer caught in the false life of mortal despair, so that the eternal may fill his being as a replenishing source of spiritual nourishment. Suffering for the Immortalae is not a spiritual/mental problem, it is only a circumstantial problem of physical/natural occurrence with worldly issues to which he is indifferent to its outcome, because of the peace of the eternal within. He must not attempt to control. He desires no effect in the world except what transpires in the moment, he has no desire and no control over the manifestation of the spirit in circumstance. He will not experience suffering except by accepting what actually transpires, that is, he is not judgmental toward circumstance. When he is regenerated in eternal spirit, he can predict the manifestation of the spirit, and his work in the world will anticipate the world, and he will be faster than they are because he can predict the manifestation of the spiritual realm. The end of mortal choice is the beginning of eternal life and immortality, or it is the limit by which a mortal can choose. As said, eternal choice is to choose with the essence of a pure self (not a false representation of self) that is no longer divided in mortal whims. It is the essence in Immortalaeism of the hero, which is divine, eternal virtue arising from within his being. The eternal virtue will fill his spirit and save his mind and belief from the emanations that are in the world that seek his allure. He will no longer survive by the methods of the world in the spirit. The limiting of a mortal life is by intellect, virtue, spirituality, or physicality and survival. To know the limiting of these subjects in mortality is death.

The ninja, the immortalae, and the hero should all consider the arrest of society to control these issues as a sign of concern for his own life and well being. Society must not be the place where he finds his acceptance, society is dead in many ways, and he must throw off the influence of society and lose his societal mind so that he can understand the martial way of the ninja, and the way of immortality. Society proclaims many things, but it limits him and only allows him through its desires and potential. The object of society in-itself, in the mind of the Immortalae, must be moved and removed permanently, so that he can see his life in its true objectivity.

In finding immutability, the world will become new when this is performed. He will begin to see his effect throughout all of time, and he will intentionally choose what he knows will be his for all time. The world is no longer an enigma, the only enigma left is his being, and the fulfillment of it in an unchanging and never-ending state. In order to solve the world, he must not play its game, he must not play the game of mortals and death, and the entanglements of personality and the identification of his self with things such as forms or paradigms or eras or wealth or sects and cults or idols, which are all dead forms. He needs to find his peace with all things by eschewing them from within himself, to be the iconoclast of his false personality, and to eschew the world, so that he is not propelled by its patterns and controlling spirits. He must not control anything, and he must have nothing that controls him. He must leave all things in their allure (all desire in the world), and he must free his personality so that his being is without encumbrance.

Part II

All of your knowledge of yourself is expressed as your turn over in your mind what constitutes your life forever, and what is only from fleeting desire which you have known until now. Why do you never change? What lasts forever in your choices? Why do you stand the test of time, and not perish with mortal whims and beliefs and desires? When you begin to speak Immortally an Eternally, you will see the world part in front of your confidence and your knowledge. They will acknowledge that you speak of something that they have not faced, and it will break them to know that you can speak so powerfully as all that they have amounted perishes before the sound of your eternal words, burnt up like chaff when the Eternal and Immortal understandings compare with their nonsense and death.

I further realize that the world of death fades, and my immortal eyes are awakened. The world of death perishes, is burnt to a cinder, and fades from memory. The never-ending is in the world, in all of its elements, but the constructs that are built instead are only temporary. As death fades, I begin to conquer evil much faster and formidably. Underneath the modern and perishing world, are Eternal and Immortal understandings and a flame burning that lies beyond the flame of life that is only temporal. Mortals satisfy and burn all of their lives in the temporary flames of life and death. Beyond that fire lies a flame of Eternal Life, and beyond that Immortal Life, and to use these fires means that one has accomplished the problem of death and decay. Death is a problem that is complimentary to all that is temporal. It is death and destruction and decay that reduce buildings and lives to nothing but dust and ash. To see past death is a great gift of insight, because it reduces death to only a temporary problem, but with the knowledge of what is Eternal and Immortal, you may begin to realize what is the solution to death, and what the solution is, I have pronounced in my book Immortalaeism. To begin to consume your life in the flames of the Eternal and Immortal, means that you are looking from the flame of mortality, and igniting the flame of the Eternal. The Immortal Self does not need anything that belongs to another, in order to find immortal fulfillment, in this manner he is free to unite with another immortal that seeks the same destiny, Double-Dragon.

If not for death, what would people become if they were to live Eternally? Most people live in cyclical patterns of life and are caught in the vice of boredom and complacency and distractedness, triviality. This sloth like attitude is what prevents people from receiving benefice. Once something is accomplished in the work of someone's life, then life will change positively. Eternal and Immortal living is impossible to these people, because they live in patterns of life that by nature are mortal, they exist in repetition, with some improvement. The end for them arrives exceedingly quickly in relationships because they arrive at the same conclusion faster each time. That can be a positive thing as well as a negative thing, as you are choosing how you learn and respond to the events in your life. Immortals and Eternals will not see life end because of dissatisfaction or death. They will instead see the projection of their Eternal and Immortal life before them, without the problems of mortality, and they will not lose vitality or zeal, or purpose or commitment, they will not be despondent or desultory, and they will not graduate to despair, they will not be conformed to caprice. They will fulfill their life's purpose by choosing to fulfill their Eternal and Immortal ways in the supreme knowledge of self. They will bring the increased vitality and increased strength and when they have routed the effects of death in their lives they will be full of promise and insight, and an individuality of fixed self with the exuberance of life will bring them never-ending satisfaction in the world. The self, in an eternal condition is capable of life without death and without the actions that bring death in the cosmos. Without interruption and decay of consciousness and spirit, the self can prosper continuously, indefinitely. Eternal virtue is the reformation of the entire being.

Some Problems of Mortality and Heroism are:
1. Uncertainty of Self and Cause
2. The problem of Death
3. Uncertainty of Providence
4. Temporal Meaning
5. Many sources of Guidance
6. Temporal Desire
7. Wastefulness
8. Regret

9.   Falseness / Truth and Untruth
10. Cyclical Patterns
11. Desire / Want
12. Disillusionment Due to Death

Mastering one's decision to choose the value of innocence, avails the truth of the being to identity. Consequently, having chosen the self, he finds that the world gives him a genuine offer. Capriciousness and doubt will never yield the proper result when someone is selecting in life. Selecting either good or evil will eventually yield the full branch of virtue, selecting both is delay. Now you are no longer wasting time, now you are eternal and immortal, and you have no longer any need for evils. Now that you are deciding what you believe in the world, the world is ready to bring you to the fate of a man that knows who he is and chooses himself. Now the hero will die knowing what he meant to the world.

The choice of being an Immortal self in the world, or Eternal, will place you over the world. Without death haunting you, and knowing yourself, all that is left for you to do at this point is simply to go out and live the paths of your life and purposes in the world. With the dichotomies of self and good and evil accomplished, and knowing your Eternity and Immortality, you will feel compelled that you are larger and more complete that most people, and that they have trivialities that withhold them from pronouncing greater freedoms and greater growth. Their growth is strangled by an unharmonious balance of the questions in life, which I have ordered and aligned rightly in this work. The mortals are burdened with many sorrows, and they have been knocked down and cannot rise because they are only thrown about in the valleys of decision, and know only temporary satisfactions such as work and essential things and the invitation of death. You will be without these problems. Guilt and shame and lies and delusion will be cut off, and the eternal light will feed his progress. You are free from their errancy, and instead of partaking in their bondage, you see only that you are much stronger than they are, and where they are sorrowing, you are viewing an emancipation of your issues, and their great grief, if it were your problem, it would be diminished because it does not actually reach you, because your resilience has actually increased, and so has your strength, and so has your ability to make the complex world simplicity - all of these increased in the size of your person when you were given to become eternal or immortal. The immortal will understand the demonic and religion, he will understand the fall and the effects of vice and sin in the spirit. He will fight against a disparaging world, and demonic, that dies from the sickness of vice and concupiscence. The world cannot hit you as it used to, because you are over the world's problems. The world and its trivialities will come and pass, but the Immortal life with you will prevail Eternally, and they will eventually be abated. The truth of your being is what is most important now. Even in the view of others and responsibilities, it is actually the truth of your being that is most private and concerning to you, and what your being will unfold and unlock to you in order to show you more about what you are meant for. It is simple to see now, that death will not hit us very hard.

The world is a supply chain, simply a chain of death and temptation, that with it I can create my own perfection, in the eyes of what I can amount in the world. I can fashion whatever I need from the world, and I know that it bears the resemblance of my Eternal and Immortal needs. My Immortal life is compatible with the world, but all things are temporary in the world. The wheel of fortune is ever spinning, and to accept an eternal and immortal life, is to win a fortune of veritas.

It is divine to say that the end of death is the end of mortality, and that by divine law, the end of wanting cures slavery and brings mortal justice and virtue.

Immortality, to those who can accept it, are borne out of blood. The sin of the human race was a divine sin, that has caused all of the vice and the problem that they can neither understand the madness of it within them, and neither can they understand how to achieve society without it. This is the death of the world, it is in covetousness. This is the crux of intellectual discussion, the behaviors of the different kinds of mortals and their ideologies. In the emergence from mortal behavior, is a new truth, that of EXITER, in becoming eternal. The truth beyond mortality is the never-ending, where will, self and life last forever. In this, is producing such a will, is IMMORTALAEISM, and there is dragon meditation to assist without coveting, and watching the impulse of the influence of the world, as demons try to affect his willpower. He must have no attachment except the self realized as eternal. In this, he will strengthen his willpower, and he will learn to resist the demonic. He must avoid the worlds influence, as does the ninja, and society will not be a part of his spiritual life. When the centre of the being is no longer located in evil, his power increases because that willpower is now available to his sphere in righteousness, because the two are mutually opposed.

Obtaining Eternal Virtue

Death is heavy in its layering of mortal dead forms in the world and in his consciousness. The consciousness of the people is corrupt, and the False Self (the Ego) seeks to rule him, and he has used these forms (dead forms) to construct his mental/spiritual identity. Underneath the dead spiritual realm of mortals and the fall of humanity is the self that does not create its identity from dead spirits (the False Self vs. the Eternal Self). This is the Eternal Self within, that has been losing its battle in the world because the will of man has fed his spirit with spiritual dead forms and intellectualisms and identities that do not allow the Eternal Self to prevail in truth in his being. He must be realized (the Eternal Self). The eternal truth cannot be realized while giving place to any desire that seeks to allure him. His being must be cleared of all death in mind, desire, and feelings, as the eternal cannot be revealed in the presence of dead forms and spiritualities and intellectualisms. The flow of death within must be stopped and controlled by him with his will, and he must choose the Eternal to be the victorious virtue and presence within so that in his spirit would be eternal life, and not unending death. He must pursue a pure consciousness undistracted, and eternal time that is not distracted by the many places that the spirit could be, so that his mental prospects of subject and form, past and future objectively become obstacles because they are occupied by the distractedness of the unregenerated mental identity/problem, which is diabolical in preventing him from seeing the Eternal while keeping him occupied with dead idols. He must eschew incessant thinking, compulsive thinking and the seduction of his mind. This is the societal mind, the one that has been given to him, it is death and lust and idolatry. His False Self has been living within him, but this self is opposed and incompatible with his eternal virtue and Self. They cannot both occupy the same mind and spirit at the same time, as virtue cannot be in the place of vice. He must win the fight to live in his Eternal Virtue. He must glimpse the Eternal within, and he will understand how to view the poison and corruption and death that has infected the world. As the Orbs of the Knowledge and Power of Good and Evil, the Eternal Virtue never has agreement with Eternal Death, and they do not understand one another. When one is present, the other is vacant, and they never coincide. He must free his mind from the Orb of Evil and Death and stop oscillating between them.

Obtaining Immortal Virtue

He must accept himself without covetousness, and he must know his Eternal place throughout time, and the things that he does, and his character and being, and his practices and how he will develop as an individual. He must stand the test of time, knowing his own fate and destiny by producing them with his decision. He wins his place by knowing who he is, so that the knowledge of self becomes first before all things, before all things in the cosmos, he becomes his own prime. As a simple object, he has only a few functions or ways that he could ever be, and he will not change. He must then allow the being (*esse*) of all things to exist as they are, he must not tempt to change them. The existence of all things are to be untouched, so that he can prove as Immortalae that he is in control of being an arbiter and a guardian, not a proponent of change, but he brings the spirit and the essence of his power and Immortality to the causes that are against the inherence of his being, this is the object of Immortalaeism, to produce heroes that coincide with civilization and its purposes, but are not meant to change it, he must harmonise being a Guardian with the causes of Immortalaeism and life itself and civilization, so that his balance and his calling in life is to face his true enemies. Lastly, he must not desire anything that tempts him, in essence, this is all things, and not only those that he finds most distracting. He must leave all temptation, and abide without its persuasion. He must only select what truly belongs to him, and find joy in being himself, and he will develop a deep inner peace in the sight of all things. In his immortality, he must understand the way things are, especially for the human race. There is only one way for things to be, and he must understand what that is. The square, the circle and the triangle of humanity and that of the cosmos, so that he understands generally what is possible for men and women. What is known in human behaviour (the square), possibilities of the universe (the circle), and the hierarchies of the cosmos and all things, the categories and sets and ranks and files and orders (the triangle). The diagram is a device that measures mastery in his respective fields of knowledge and understanding.

Normalism

Normal Heroism

Normal is what is sensible in the world and cosmos that pertains to all of the needs of a healthy individual. Society's role is to establish normalcy, from a way of life, which we produce in agreement. Normalcy is regulated, consistent and persistent, practical, efficient, dependable and sound. Thus, normalcy is regarded. The memorandums are full, and the full merit of life has been expressed. Society is in the pendulum between success and error. To change the way of life, the provision must be for the majority, but Immortalaeism is not for the majority and does not seek to change society. We are champions of virtue. As champions of virtue, we understand that law is to govern after a method of rule, and that justice in essence is to never offend (whereas moral is the dialectic of voluntary rule against subordination). Justice, being a virtue, is fulfilled by virtue itself, and virtue is validity of character, and virtue is the fulfillment of many claims.

A champion of our failures and miseries must rise, the epitome of our successes, and none of our grief's. He must conquer the problems of many. He is a champion of the people, and the fruition of our labors. If this hero is successful in morality and justice, then he will be self-motivated and assertive in the conversation of our politics, but he will understand that what he accomplishes is without hypocrisy, and for that he may adventure that he is the most valid participant as overcoming our problems, most dignified. Where he fights, and where he is pitted, though not entangled out of mere subjection and inclusion by his own problems, we must decide that he is providing the most evident knowledge of what is intrinsically, the fight of us all, and for a right cause. He stands before us all and he will use his soul and spirit to overcome his conflicts, and not a reward for it all, but furtherance. What can society afford such a hero? He gives his life, but he is not a part of governmental authority, like a knight, he truly knows no greater lord than himself, because his will is beyond mortal evils, and he must rule his own beliefs and procure the destination of his soul, and in this, society will be admonished with the personal life of a hero, with a personal victory to achieve, so it is a personal vendetta for the hero.

To see failure and to offer conjecture would make him a politician, but he sees all of societies failures, and in this he is alone because he has none of their imperfections. He will rise against oppression, hypocrisy and tyranny and failure and temptation, and he will seek to throw down their sources demonstratively in physicality. The consequence is that it will be the theory of the hero's life against the theories of the despots, or the evils, and because it is also in theory, his victory may perhaps be a victory for all of society. In vain he could see his life coming to an end without opposing the evils that have beset him and his people. Wastefulness beseeches their time, all the more they use it with insufficiency, as cupidity and luxury do much to deter our hero, ignoring that which plagues his mind and spirit, and society. His virtue succeeds their lust and civility, and he proves their ideals, but they do not imagine him, they imagine themselves.

. He never understood the way of society, because he could not understand a life of complacency, where the times rush by in domestication, because he understood the nature of conflict in the world. He was a warrior within, and the guide of his life was his spiritual understanding and source, and it was his way as a warrior and a fighter, and it is invigorated by the fierceness of his belief. Why do we fight and war? What satisfies our fight? What makes us wrong? Universal means application everywhere, which means to a warrior that he must be able to fight in the world anywhere, and be successful, that he may venture into different battlefields, and that the possibilities are without end. His fight is universal.

He needs to learn to oppose with his spirit and body. He must see his intellectualism as his fist. The way to fight never changes, he must learn the categories of fighting, such as punch, kick, block, throw, redirect, deflect, reverse, grapple, sweep kick, round house, parry etc. In the animus, the divisions of possible action are divided into metaphysical categories, once the categories of fighting are known, then he must see himself as a martial artist and construct his own martial art, and he must learn to develop styles of combat that suit him in his spiritual presence that connects him to the divine cosmos. The warrior desires within to be able to express himself intelligibly in a fight, and professionally, which requires the knowledge of honor codes and rulership. He faces much suppression and opposition, but he must be learned intellectually to discern that when he is offended, he understands the offense and its implication in regard to what he may or may not fight over, whether or not the offense is opposed in law. That is, he must understand fighting without the opinion of others, and he must understand that the way of fighting is that he cannot be placed in a position where he sees that he cannot live properly any longer. They are misleading and deceptive to pretend as they venture for their objectives, and he must be vigilant to watch what is happening, truly transpiring, behind the illusion of the world, and he is not unaware of the infractions against him, although they pretend and mock. The warrior that wins has either defeated his enemies, or he has won world favor, but virtue and martial arts is first, and then perhaps to fight. If ignorance reaches such a pinnacle that he is forgotten, he will be considered 'dead' from his enemies, though he guards the apple, he is treated as a slave, left for dead and forgotten. He will understand the sting of deception, and will be born again into masculinity as a renegade, a vagabond, because his will should not be broken by the opinion of another, he receives greater independence. His fortune improves, and so does his worth. He will stand in the face of any adversary, and he will not kneel or bow. He will face despotism, and tyranny that brings oppression and suppression. Tyranny brings slavery and destruction, digression against innocence, starting wars with no previous contact. It brings competition that chases the value of men to subordination through religious, intellectual and fighting causes, it does this through the limit of their expedience in the world. Tyranny can come from a god, or an angel, or a king, and comes with despotism. The tyrant strives to be the largest competitor, the wealthiest, bringing economic downfall and submission in forced labour. The tyrant will attach chains with the illusion of regular work, he introduces the influence of his empire with dependency, he will purchase the available world, sealing economic war alliances, and divide the resources of the world, and he will accept no comparison in his authority. He introduces the threat of slavery by military, economic or cultural or religious defeats. He must break the chain of the tyrant and the slave by breaking the mind of the tyrant, his arguments, policies, culture and religion. His entire dominion is false to the hero, the hero understands it as simply false, and nothing else. The unjust adjure the same habits, by attaching chains underneath the visible society, in order to control the people. So, the hero must be highly opinionated so that he may see above the criminal and the tyrant's empire, or any other adversary, and he must be the most proficient at fighting. These adversaries are all present in the world at all times, it is in this that the hero proves his divinity, because he understands and opposes transgression that is eternal, or divine in wickedness. His faithful companion is virtue, and in this, he may dissolve the lies of tyranny, and all the subtleties of society.

Power

The Shaping of Power

There is no power for those that do not contend with the threat of death. Power is the vigor and energy of the hero. Immortality is his vitality. Power is the spiritual force of the machination of his understanding, and of his spirit and being. Power is the only thing that is real in fighting, and nothing else. Power his held in the spirit, in the development of spiritual power, and spiritual power draws the connection to anything that may be affecting him in the spiritual realm. Spiritual power in this way is awareness, usually through meditation, and heights of awareness are possible in transcendence, the spirit and power are the life that fills with presence, and also the connection to the spiritual realm. The definition of power in Immortalaeism is that power is the energy field of spirit that surrounds all things, it is the constitution of its entity. In this, power is the accomplice of eternal life and immortality in the spiritual realm. The word that I have created from Immortalaeism's language for universal power by entity and matrix is 'CO', meaning universal power, and 'COAE', meaning universal powers, every from first precedence. There is no one that understands that power will be the only understanding that makes him accomplish his enemy, because they do not understand there is no other way, and that power will accomplish it, and nothing else. Power will guide the hero. There is freedom in power, and there is assurance and victory. The source of power will determine the kind of ability. There is no other, there is only power. There is no way, there is only power. There is no truth, there is only power. There is no divinity, there is only power. There is no weakness, there is only power. Power is the fulfillment of life. To be filled with power, he must find his self-realized identity that is without encumbrance or difficulty, the spirit that overcomes with victory. Power governs in spheres of expression. In the criminal's power, he accepts that he has violated safety, and the governance and his conscience then seek conviction, which is the power to perform no harm, which places his hands and body in a position of inability. The rule of personal power, is that the opposite of what you believe could occur, if it is transgressed. In this regard, we shape and determine our experience. By the forms of experience that we live in, according to their power, determines our experience. A higher form of existence comes through belief. The rule that what one does to someone else could happen to them is permissible, because the extended action, then becomes an invitation. It is proper to fully form a sphere of dominion and master it, or else the consciousness of one's mistakes will pull him down from advancing to a new sphere of power, because he has the ramifications of transgression that are pending. Power explains all actions and their reasons. There is no other way. He must allow himself to think differently, so that he can allow for new dominion. The intelligence of one's dominion can be expressed in the inscription of a ring to design the pattern of will and dominion. These are symbols of power and dominion, calculations of the spirit. The will must be taught permanency in order to reach a greater power. When consistent and permanent will outperforms a hesitant will in reaching dominion, his dominion will increase, and his life will become permanent, as the permanence of profession elicits a payment. Words are spiritual commands, and every word has a spiritual consequence that is interpreted by powers. Internal spiritual power is the inner source of the outward signs, the body, and the domain. In power, by understanding power, he can understand the communication of the military, as a corporeal body that speaks as one and takes command, because all dominion and power that is the same works in agreement. In order to develop more power, one must accept that he negates power by his performance to power. In this, he will understand power and its conveyance toward him, and he will understand that power can be called and is given to perfection. He will become powerful if he does not tempt power, but allows power to increase itself to him. When he does this, he will be accepted by power because he understands when power acts that his intelligence is proven.

The stages of power determine his expression, and governance and achievement. Power will become what anyone thinks, only they will not understand power unless they can see the domain that they are in, and how it operates. Power fashions after the correct or incorrect responses from dominion, and it does not favor, or select that one should aspire or perish. He does not understand power, but he understands that the world is governed, and that the tables of mans domain and being are compatible with the world. We see that many do not understand how to accomplish furtherance, but they do understand the difference between progress and regression. They cannot be in the place of power, and accept that they should not be in the governance of progress, as they will not be acceptable in the world, because of competition. They will never understand progress if they do not believe in the possibilities of power. The power of death is regression and fall, and it is at times upon accomplishment that someone chooses regression, due to lack of discipline, and their error is apparent. The truth of power is that power will accept someone for what he deserves, but not more or less. The power of covetousness is becoming of the power of tyranny, and it has a different dominion than the power of a justice. The power of covetousness is the power of the lie, the lie brings subordinance and death. The deficiency of unmerited approval and false concourse brings shame and slavery, and it is a false ego that seeks this approval, which is contaminable to the progress of the spirit.

The problem with power is that many do not understand power, and they do not understand how to be powerful. It is admirable to be powerful, and it will be the only thing that displays the progress of a lifetime. Power is in all success, and all successfulness is the wisdom of power, thus, power will be the first thing that someone needs in life, and it is the beginning and the end of a lifetime. The hero must understand power first, and he must understand that his opportunity is the only thing that he has to be victorious, because of his way in the world. The power of the hero can be manipulated and esoteric and high forms of power can be reached, in the accomplishment of task, there is spiritual reward, and in the accomplishment of the hero's life, he will gain reward from his victories, and this wisdom from his challenges and victories will shape his state as a warrior, and he will be given a higher place because his knowledge is the knowledge of invincibility and victory. The hero will have power because he will understand that his challenges are the problems of his understanding, and he will understand that he is capable of accomplishing his objective because he is capable of understanding great power.

The power of justice is in the affect of a dominion, but justice is not that profitable without the entirety of virtue and success. Justice decrees that whatever effects its dominion may be affected in return, to the same degree of power. Divine justice is to never be incorrect in regard to the spirit, which is far more accurate and formidable than institutional justice. Divine justice regards the purpose of man, his existence, and his need for spiritual accountability, and that the denominations of voluntary choice bring lasting eternal, spiritual effect, and that the powers that govern such things are governing man's spirit, and for this there are religions and gods. In Immortalaeism, the purpose is power, immortality, and heroism. Enlightenment is a part of spirituality, and can be found through the grails, and it helps us to see clearly according to the spirit, and it is a spiritual gift that is suited under Dragon meditation. The enlightened sees through the spiritual darkness of the world, according to the terrain of the spirit, and he understands how not to be in the impulsive patterns of the world, and neither is the eternal or the immortal convinced or bound by the impulsive patterning of society. The immortal must realize his self immortally, his unmanifested being, and he must accustom a clear depiction of himself and his own image in how he views himself, which is the image of the essence of his immortal self, and he must realize it and it must become the field of energy that emanates from him, which is his power, of the unmanifested spirit. The mind of the mortal world is searching for meaning, and they have not understood more than the egoic self. The way of the immortal is born out of necessity, and not out of desire. Necessity is clean, and desire is unclean. He must watch at the portico of his spirit for desire, and he must make it leave, so that he is not impulsive, or demonic or superfluous. He must select things that come from the power of his spirit, from the intelligence of his unmanifested self, and from this self, he develops his life as an immortal. It is a life that cannot be tempted, because it was not made with temporal understandings of passing society. He obtains power by communing with his unmanifested self, and discovers the true channels of his power to his being, and not the superficiality that is in ideas and intellectualisms, but the real proponents that empower him and cause his spirit to thrive. He should have inner peace at all times of ancillary, and he is not moved by the world. The spiritual powers of the world challenge and attempt to dominate and control, but the Immortalae must be vigilant and awake, so that he is always controlling his own destiny. He is perpetually in meditation, to experience immortality, he finds meditation navigating and preparing his spirit. When manifested, then power is adorned. He is in contemplation against the world, and in this, he must be successful, he must understand the Dragon.

Leader

Basic Identity

Mastery of self in private intelligence and how the cultivations of apperception are suitable and compliant with a hero and the resemblances are as in similitude to legend, myth, tale, story, and illustration in the process of becoming, aligned with aptitudes and personality, with a particular intelligence which resides within, is a particular knowledge which I will reveal.

The potential of self is an issue of personality, aptitude and behavior. As is suitable for the Immortalae, the hero is well developed in skill, in belief, in common interest and personal interest, in contending, in education. He understands the edifice of human development and rule. All qualities have a place, quantifiably, which accords with ruler-ship, which is the expression of human characteristic, which is the categories of that which is the 'most-able'. Heroes are the most apt in fighting. Heroes possess great spiritual strength, and mental prowess, including rule and governance. Immortalae will view these qualities as examples of the strongest and the most capable among men. It is the strength of men that wills everything, and it is the prowess of men that determines everything. Heroes undertake the full burden, and they do not divert from responsibility and duty. The hero shoulders challenges and they are victorious in overcoming them all, and this is the end of man, because he has fully accepted the burden of what to accept, and he has gone further. The end is the end of his civilization and there is nothing beyond that, except in the mind. They are finished with the virtues of masculinity and maturity, and there is nothing wanting in their personality, and they have not accepted corruption of consciousness. They possess an inner talent with virtue to understand how to accomplish internal challenges and mental challenges. In developing personality, and accomplishing its limits, he narrows his fate by selecting that which will not change, within himself. In this, he will begin to develop high opinion, higher than most, and he disappears from their minds, and they cannot suspect him, because of what he understands. He will be the one that will not trespass though he is not a solider or guard, but he will find that he is in the most suitable position in order to find an enemy because he does not believe in anything except that he is the one that understands where to find an adversary because he is always understanding of their behavior, and the criminal, because it is open before him, and he will find eventually that his courage and prowess will lead him to an enemy. His fate is chosen, unless he defects from it. He will understand that in order to be in the place of a hero, he needs to be within his own life, and that his life is becoming the place of a hero.

Before he understands that he is a hero, he will naturally face the approval of several tests. The edifice of his mind is one, his great belief is two, his mental prowess and intelligence and character is three, combat ability is four, his understanding of virtue and the social and the world (wisdom) is five, his devotion is six, how he deals with temptation is seven, accomplishments and experience is eight. He may be confirmed by a deity or an angel, or he may be given gifts, something that confirms his new status. The Immortalae face no choice but to be masterful in these said areas, and with the confirmation of personality the cosmos avails its confirmation of such a needful man. Now that he understands that his work may be worth gold, though he denies mammon, he is able to understand how to evaluate his economy. He has become a hero, and is no longer a common man, and his intelligences and his being have progressed, due to his great belief, and the fashioning of great character. The Immortalae may be dark, and gruesome, and mean and difficult, and reserved, but they will be honorable, and they will understand how to be heroes.

As a citizen, you must cooperate with the law of the land. You must regulate your time in a predictable manner, which regulates living for all. The predictability of human nature and what is needed is the same through time. Now you must regulate, because your time is beyond theirs, and your must be the one that understands how to accomplish being a hero, because you are the one that is a hero, and there is no other that will be a hero if you are not one. This is not arrogance, the hero is not prideful. The hero is striking at the heart of the issues, to end them, and he is not regulating instances of difficulty. His vendetta is signaled with lawlessness by the approval of gods and deities, that he must be the one that will accomplish his difficulty and that there is no other that will take his place. This understanding reaches back to preliminary societies, that naturally, there is no rule, and that all men are free from governance and the chains of social compacts. But he must be excellent at fighting, and this is a necessary credential of the Immortalae.

Men's paths are not equal, none have the same fate. The hero will hear his own calling, and he will make a place for the call, and it will become his office and administration. The hero must not use the artifice of the world and its tales and legends to cancel his mind over his individual place. In heroism, the hero cannot be followed, and it is more preferable that he creates his place out of originality. He will become something, after enough experience has allowed that he receive the name of hero, in the world. The implements that he has should be his instruments of war, he should not seek anything unless it comes to him, and he will be the centre of his own life. He must use what is available to exercise himself, and not an artificial progress, and he will be guided to a sustainable and original origin for his place in the world. He must break the barriers of his own progress, and work hard at becoming strong and refined and intelligent. He must develop after his own personality and intelligence, and he will not be illegitimate or temporary, or subject to failure or inadequate or erroneous. He must have all original things. His advanced traits and personal conditioning will take him to the height of civilization, and beyond it. The spheres of power, talent, eternal life, immortality, meditation, guardianship, martial arts and heroism.

He may follow many things in the world, such as economy, or news, or society, or others, or books, except he only needs Immortalaeism, but he will understand his destiny, he will not be misled. He will never become a hero by corrupting himself with shallow agreements. A hero needs to learn how to fight for causes, he needs to learn spirituality, justice and equanimity, slavery and freedom and tyranny and war.

Reason is the display of the wisdom of the hero, and it is the refinement of the hero's treatment of how he understands the world, through the perspective of his beliefs and power. He will understand the world by the virtues of heroism, and he does not understand many reasons and paradigms in the world, and he understands what he thinks about them. Unlike many leaders, he does not display knowledge often, but he fights with it. He is an academic and an intellectual leader, and his way of thinking is strong and sometimes informal, because it is linked to his way of combat and victory. He does not understand that people are not sufficiently reasonable, and he has no hypocrisy, though many do have hypocrisy. He is the foremost, and his quality is beyond compare. His reason will take him across the world, and it will make him the most selected, because he will understand how to deal with civilizations, because that is his occupation. He needs training in logic and patterns, because to be able to think and reason independently, and develop knowledge, which is more useful that learning and retaining knowledge. He will understand how to solve enigmas, and how to solve the worlds enigmas, and he will understand the world in its entirety. His sensibility, evaluation, and conclusion/decision process is without interference or hesitation, and he is decisive. Through meditation he has mastered his temperament and presentation, so that in exuberance and without impunity from an adversary he will keep his mind focused from his true meditative position.

The hero's ability will be precise and decisive. He will be perfect in warfare, a warrior of repute, and the abilities of a hero are various. In sabotage, he may understand how to attack and disappear. The hero should understand divinity and deities. The hero should understand different civilizations. He may be exceptional with weapons. He should understand war, and siege. He should understand the use of the supernatural. He should understand fire and explosives. He should understand tactics. He should understand defense. He should understand varying odds and numbers of men in combat. He should understand his opponent. He should understand other types of warriors. He should understand warriors, and the different offices of society, such as wisdom. He should understand men and women. He should understand spiritualism. He should understand strategy. He should understand armies. He should understand terrain. He should understand dissimulation. He should understand non violent attack, such as knowledge. He should understand prophecy.

The hero should be reserved, and reserved strength. The manner should be that he does not understand the provocation of impress, or seeking favor. He should be cold and dark and serene and masculine and cultured and clean and well educated. He should carry honor, and deep respects. He should understand his honor, and it will keep him safe, and he will understand what to think of his opponent. His honor is how he understands his own dignity, in regard to himself and the world. They will not be in the place of the hero, so will not understand that they will speak to him but he does not understand, because his high stature will place him against many opponents and he will be in a position of leadership. His leadership and his high place will not give respects to those that do not understand his place in combat. He will attempt to understand the leadership, and he will respect their responsibility, and he will work with them on the problems of guardianship, or the state or society. His presence should be reserved and darkly cast, and of fierce countenance. He will understand how to be a professional warrior, and he will have an honorable presence, of confidence. The hero should hold no guilt in his conscience, as he properly understands his domain within society. Guilt and shame are foreign to Immortalae, who are given to respect and honor. They will not understand a blasphemous mind and conscience. He must respect that which deserves credit, and he must give honor to that which he holds dignified with integrity and honesty.

The merits of a hero are the accomplishments for which he gains respect and occupation. They are the accolades of his trade, and that for which he earns the regard of the leadership. The hero will be tested in order to understand what he may achieve, and his merits will hold that he can rule adversaries. The hero will be instrumental in his office. He must accomplish the full rank of leadership in many spheres, including fighting and war, because he must cross civilizations.

Insignia

Elect

He will make the devil scream and he can go through Hell, and search though your region to find ways to combat forces of darkness or demons if he chooses to, and be associated with demonic war. The land has fallen, and we need a hero to find out what has happened to us. The signs of heroism are in the occupation. Bravery and courage are required, and you must take on the form of war. A weapon of choice, an evil, wicked opponent, the sign of learning and progress, and spiritual victories.

Leadership is a blessing, and if progress is offered it should not be neglected, so we accept that to become a hero is progress, and that much of civilization may not amount to his understanding. The incidence that one should respond appropriately and reasonably in the circumstance of evil is normal to most citizens, and many would not ask for a hero, but we understand that his knowledge and capability is better for us than asking a regular guard to administer to the problem. He must dismiss the inhibitions of the times, and low behavior, and reserve honor and respect, and his quest emerges, to reach a resting place, and blessing, through great ambition. The symbol of the hero is that he must leave society, and find his real challenges in life, and in breaking societal understandings, he will become himself. He begins to accommodate such things in his personality as, 'great strength', 'greater than most', 'prodigy', 'savior', 'gifted', 'justified', 'angelic of war', 'god of war'. Mentally and spiritually, he is no longer the same as other people. His ambitions and beliefs brought an epiphany, which was the realization of self. By truth in the circumstance he accepted the decision that he was different, independent, and through the scrutiny of Immortalaeism, he was revealed as a hero. The hero then begins to realize that the mind of society is a barrier, and he will think beyond them, and he will take his station as a guardian. The hero is well favored, he is given to intellectualism, law and war and spirituality. The hero is masculine, clean and strong and cultured. He bears an insignia, which is divine, cosmic and world-wide immortal-hero. These are the men and women that have defeated mortality, out of the worlds travail and the blood of sinful death, they have come for the fight of the earth, they have an astral sign and path. Immortalaeism raises the standard.

Icon

Unique

The icon is an opportunity for all Immortalae, and within Immortalaeism, it is a way of summing his endeavor so that he is known properly. The icon is a name that is above reproach, a representative of a thing in its epitome. The icon of the hero is a conceptualized artwork that displays the immortality of human endeavor, in combat with the cosmic, divine and the worldly. The world has not been given the opportunity to understand the icons because they do not understand that there is no way of making them appear unless the icons are able to understand the public, and the icon of Immortalae do not seek public approval. There is no place for them because they do not believe in the icons, because they do not understand how to accommodate their excellence, and they will not believe in them, because they are only able to be a part of something that is not a part of society. That is why I am an icon and desire to be a hero, because I understand that there is no way except that my talents will take me to the same place as an icon, as a hero and I will not be apparent to society. There is no hero in society and no icon, except for/towards children, because they think that they are the people that understand how to perform cosmic and divine and worldly action, but that they are incapable of finding them because the preliminary work of intelligence and fashioning is not done by society. They will never understand a hero or an icon, because they do not understand the possibility. The hero and the icon must prevail without society's approval, because they do not use the limitations of society. The hero is displayed to the welcome of the public, and they trust the hero because he understands them, but they do not trust the hero to tempt him by committing their trust, and the hero must not accept it from them.

The hero has great strength, special ability, intellectual prowess, muscular, and great alignment to a cause, identity as a martial artist and god of war, and a weapon and armor that are in alignment with his mental understandings, the mentality of fighting and martial arts. This is done in accordance with the nature of conflict, and opposing views, of which the hero is capable of rejecting, which attests to his intellectualism and his representation.

In comparison to the era of the crusades, it is important to note that the grail is the subject of a knight's quest in previous times, and that Exiter and Finality are both grails. The quest is an icon that symbolizes an over-arching mission, or a search for something of great significance. The lore and symbolism that surrounds quests and knighthood are high, and what is high must be learned by Immortalae. Immortalaeism is of high stature, and those that are of Exiter and Finality must be able to be representatives of the Spirituality, or else they must recline until they are approved. I have fashioned the warrior of the grail in Immortalaeism, and I have specified who he is and how he arrives in the world (Immortalaeism III). The Immortalae will all progress into lasting ways, and they will be as unique and exemplary as the icons of books, games, comics, *legends* and stories.

Concept Hero

Heroism, Our Profession

There are seldom any concept-games that are not actually possible in real life. The context and plots are different, but the game is real. The concept-game is an opportunity to see an advertisement for warriors, for Immortalae. There are no opportunities for warriors and heroes, but there are many for doctors or engineers, in Immortalaeism we view the concept hero as our advertisements and it makes sense because no one cares, because no one cares about the electronic hero, and no one cares about us. In the end, the concept hero is the only hero that makes sense to Immortalae, and the only lifestyle, because they will never understand who I am, because I don't understand them either, it makes sense that he is a concept hero, because that is what makes him think about who he is. There are no concept heroes, except all of the heroes in concept are real in life because they are true to their circumstance as an oracle, and that is part of what Immortalae is, which is that we are a part of a greater conference of Immortal heroes that seek to fully master and understand heroism. The only hero that makes sense is a warrior hero, because he does not find anything except danger in all that he does. He will understand that he is a hero, because he understands the insignia, and he will employ himself into fitness at all times to be ready for the opponent, and he understands there is no one except him that can call his responsibility in life, and what it matters to him. He will be in the place of a secret society as eternal and immortal, and will believe in what they do, and as Immortalae, he will make war across the world. He understands what is in the problem of the world, and he understands how he needs to be involved in what takes place in the world.

Electronic games hold excellent possibilities for Immortalae, that the Immortalae have satisfaction in performing, from their natural generation. They will understand that I am one, because I can present the same spirituality / mentality in actuality, and the hero has come to life in the flesh. There is no one in the world that can stop it, and there is freedom in performing the circumstances of concept game heroes. We are free because society is not involved in the combat. The way that I get satisfaction is by being completely free from the informal agreements of society, and I do not believe in what society decrees in entirety. The concept heroes are to be entertaining for the Eternals and Immortals, something that reflects the vigor of their heroism, and the commitment that temporal life is over and that they will never change, and the infinite self will reveal the immutable self, and in the consultation of ideological personalities that are fully committed to warriorism, they may see semblance. We are always looking to engage in the action of heroism, our sport, and the opportunity that concept-games present display a multitude of implications where Immortalae would see their involvement, where the usefulness of heroism is in full play.

Immortalae may not only venture their talents outside of society, they may also play integral roles in such offices as law or military or politics. As Guardians of Civilization, they must decide where they think the best suit is, in their coming conflict in the world.

Alter

Genesis of Conflict

As goodness' hierarchy descends from the apex to the base, the corruption and the method of evil ascends from the base to the apex in the realm of the good. It is a way of seething and catching what defies the standard of the good, and bringing sedition and divisiveness, and spoiling the disciplines of the good upon their people. The temptation to betray comes to the unfinished works of the good. Wherever goodness ventures, evil attempts to find a way of corrupting it, and the good destroy the works of the wicked. The simplicity of good and evil is that the selection of either is basic, and the complexity of the issue is greater. Subordination to be ruled, in opposition, is at the front of the conflict. An inferior or limited rule taxes and tempts the land into revolt, and opportunistic business finds a place among the subordinates, those who desire to see the fulfillment of their arguments. In this, the Immortalae are always in arbitration, because the rule does not accommodate for all ways of life, and the reality is difficult because they must comply with the rule, so that they cannot accomplish their way. For this, I have deemed Immortalae as those that begin from the possibility of becoming a part of command without formal governance, and they are critics of governance, and they do not betray justice, and their business begins in the streets (behind and without society). They feign that which limits their power. Immortalae may not cross the tenets of the grails. He understands the world and its fights, but he expects that eternal life and immortality will distance us from the damage of the conflict, in that he will not be divided or convinced by sedition and the breakdown of social trust. The perpetual lies of evil are poisonous and shameful and infecting, deadening its host, making it numb in certain areas. The Immortalae, in understanding eternal lies, will bring great liberation by the strength of immortality. Anti-heroes and heroes emerge and conflict brings the ultimate seeds of evil, of the problem, paradigms against paradigms. Demons and the anti-hero converge in physicality, and when they are ready to formally oppose, they will release the fullness of their demonic influence upon him and all of their doctrine and suffocated rule. The full merit and intelligence and ration of the Good opposed to its equal opposite. The nature of evil is that it does not accept the authority of anything unless it is corrupt, but truthfully, Immortalaeism has no ruler either; in the maturity of both good and evil. We subtract to mutual aims, but the anarchy and nihilism of evil suggests that to desire consistency is to develop rule, which is hated. Without harmony, the two must oppose, and without subordination, and still not meeting agreement, occasions death or permanent subordination. They simply do not wish to be ruled, because they cannot be accommodated and choose not to be. A foreign enemy will follow this argument and he will not relent to defeat until subordination or death. It is preferable that the Immortalae strike being heroes in their personal lives, because it has full agreement, because they are called *personally*. In regard to institution, if they are called to be heroes, then they do not necessarily share the fight in the same way that the institution does. Evil men can be perfectly acceptable in many ways, as long as interests are not in contention.

Civilization

The hero is not always above civilization, but he may be beyond it in understanding how civilizations perform, and he must understand what is behind civilization in the spirit. He is accessible and he may be contacted if necessary. He plays an integral role, and has a place among peoples. He is seated among the highest and most valuable in the land when he has finished his training and he is pronounced. He will understand his place, and he will become the fulfillment of a protector and guardian, and he has the opportunity to change the fate of his civilization, and the affairs of the world through the knowledge of the immortal. The world will change, and the dispensation of power and its struggle will be the event in the world, and the hero is in the centre of these actions, and he will overcome and subdue his enemy if he is victorious, and he will bring the great understandings of the times to an end. He will fight across country and terrain, against opposing civilizations and armies, and he will accomplish the problem of his life in combat. He does not believe in their methods or constructs, and he will be given the opportunity to display the fashioning of his character and purpose in the ensuing conflict. He will not believe in them, and he will not understand them, and it is the reasons of his society and civilization which have provocation and offense, and his understanding should accomplish fully his opponent, to the death and collapse of their machinations. His participation in the clandestine and secret, in the arcane and mythological, bring him into the full use of his understanding, when he understands the opposing civilization. He will be in the capital, against the capital, with the best minds, and his special knowledge will convey great worth in threat. The opposition will lead an offense and the hero will understand that his society is threatened, and that he is at war, because he understands that they are in the modus of attack. The problem is now his, and he will begin his masterpiece, for which he has waited patiently.

The Immortalae is above religion. He crosses religion at the height of deity, and he understands what religions are, and how the spirituality of the religion operates. He has climbed its use, he has view of its high men, and he has heard their words, and he has seen their alters and tabernacles and relics, and he does not care. The hero's religion is his destiny, and in that he will not be stopped. He is among the spiritually elite, and understands the digressions of the soul, and its need for treatment, and the hero understands how to treat his own soul. The souls of the many are supplicant and pious, because they have needed to understand the poverty of their spiritual circumstance, and they have designed that they will be the most ardent, because they are so needful. The religious do not understand the hero, because they do not understand his methods, as a priest does not understand how to live without a god. The priest understands the gods will toward men, and how the god appeases men for their spiritual ways, because they are lacking spiritual life and rule. The priest will be the man who says that all men should follow his god, or else they will not understand how to accept that there is no other way to honor the representation of his way of life, and that he will be the most favorable, because he understands that his way was greater because he honored a god, in that he believes that he is approved and given consent, because he has won the favor of a god. The Immortalae may win the favor of the priest because he is a liberator. The gods will provide signs, and he must be willing to accept his place, because he has accepted to approve the god of his power. The hero does not accept that it is the willfulness of a god's servant that will prove that his test in the world was won by following a god. The need of a god is that he is committed to the same problem, and in civilizations, it appears that they are. The Immortalae is the spiritually elite, and religion and gods will not improve his life or spirituality. The hero does not 'sin' in his consciousness, he simply selects whether he would like to be good or evil, because he understands the effect of sin, and he understands when he has done something to transgress, because it affects him negatively because it crosses his eternal life and immortality. The cause of the hero drives him, and there is no participation for which his deep interests are not involved. He understands gods as benefactors, and that he needs to accomplish his own divinity, instead of acting on that of another god. The cause of the hero will not be interrupted by a god, and his cause is united to his spirituality, and his spirituality he knows, will bring him to a destined end. The cause of the hero is his 'piety', and there is no semblance of his cause with another cause, and no god that should stand between him and his desired end. The continuance of his power and devotion will continue in the afterlife, because his devotion is in part with his character and personality, and he will not conform, he is immutable. Society regards many merits, but the merits of the hero are not in demand, and his spirituality is not afforded, and he understands how to fight, how to die, and how to win in combat, but these traits are sometimes overlooked, and he does not participate in his strengths in a non-combative society. Uniformity has not replaced the professionalism of the warrior in war, and the professions of the world still maintain that the office of the hero is a talent that is worth gold.

The culture of the hero is of world-wide prominence. He will understand that culture is the expression of the most impressionable and permanent values of a society, in the construction of society, it is the place of a people to construct their own values, conditions, and terms. The culture of a people is the confidence of their expression, and the opportunity to make themselves known for their identity. In relation to other cultures, culture is a private matter, and the most profitable cultures are the most influential, nevertheless, the independence of a people issues a discreet and rejected notion, in the respect of persons, that culture may not be rivaled, and the confidence and potential of the people is a private matter. Culture is the intelligence that is issued from the accomplishments of a people, in the understanding of what is common among world achievements, and what is uncommon. Culture produces a way of life, that is constructed around the identity and understanding of the people. It is not important to have culture, but to have intelligence and power. The concentration and focus and meditation of a person, and people, are the convective elements that produce culture, and in the critical mark, the stigma that they arrive at perpetually as a unique people, in the branches of understanding that they generally meet again and again in their maturity. Culture therefore, is not mandatory, and it can be created by an individual person, and it can be given to the sole respects of a family, and often those that generate culture are signaled as leaders and original icons, which is sometimes compared with societal fathers, and societal icons. The concentration of the people is the most important, and that they generate a meditated and full identity, independent and without much influence. International culture does not matter, it is the success of the individual that is necessary, and that the competition is victorious, and thus, nihilism to culture is needful, because all that is necessary is victory, and not the concourse of societal pride. The culture that is needful is intelligence and excellence and strength and power, and it is nihilism to all else. There is nothing else. One must consider his place, and his position in relation to the world, and not mind culture, and what he must perform in the world, and all else is nihilism. There is no societal standing that is more important than victory, and there is no influence that matters more than the influence of self, and self governance. There is no culture in the world that is impressive, one must be fully immersed in his culture to succeed, and all vanity is nihil. To be influenced is to fail, the influence that cannot be integrated is vanity, to be influenced is to reject the leadership of self. The stimulus of likenesses infers that one has his own way of expressing that culture, but originality is the most valuable character. The influenced character cannot be victorious, because the credit will arrive at the original, and all else is false glory. One must learn not to be influenced, and to accept the circumstance of his life, he must understand that he is responsible for the leadership and he will need the lessons that are given to him, and he will need to accept the way that is before him, and nothing else. If it is war, then he must accept fully, that there is nothing else, and to accept its full teaching. He must not be divided in his consciousness about what he does, his meditation and alignment must be whole, in that he accepts the training and the learning of a lifetime devoted to a single cause, unless it becomes something different. He must see that in order to arrive at victory, he must not understand culture, but he must understand how to navigate the problems of life, because they mean death and suppression and slavery and abuse if he is not successful. It doesn't matter what he becomes, he must accept his life's challenge. There is no champion, and there is no hero, and there is no leader, but what matters is that he understands what he must face in life, and that it is his life that matters, and not a fixation, an image, or a spiritual lust. There is no reputation that is bigger than his own life, and there is no way for him to understand what he must do, than to understand his own life. There is no cause, until he understands what he must do, and there is no success, until his leadership can convey his cause. He will not understand the world, until he understands himself, and for what reason would there be culture, if he does not understand his own life. There is no one but you because you do not understand that you are the one that must stand in the way of life and be the one that has properly understood your formation in the world, in the world's crucible. Then he will be successful, because he will realize that there is nothing else that he can do, but he must be a hero, and he must ennoble his cause by performing its reality. He will not accept the denial of self, he must accept who he is, and that it is okay for him to understand himself properly, and he will understand how he must approach the difficulty of his cause. It is apparent then, that culture does not matter, it is to accept his place in the world, and that is where his life truly is, because he understands himself, he may begin, and not because he understands culture. He will understand the true direction of his life, when he understands himself, he will find that distractions are a waste of time, and he must achieve furtherance. The objective is that he progresses spiritually to the accomplishment of a real rank, office, and title, and honor, and that is his principal objective. There are none that he must face, more than himself, and in facing himself, he becomes himself. Once understood, he must face it in the world, and he must accept his training. He will find that he can change the systems that he is in, and he understands the spiritual aspect, that some things can be changed, and some things can be manipulated or dismissed in order that he may progress, he will find that the confines of his life, the patterns and the repetition, he can change, and he will find that he does not understand why life has brought so much problem to his threshold. He must see that in facing his problem, that the ultimate evil, at this stage, is that what belongs to him is destroyed, corrupted, never brought into reality. His true spirituality has awakened, and the scales will fall off his eyes, to reveal the true world, and not the illusion of culture and influence and temporary spirits that have no real meaning. This culture, of which I speak, is of an unruled energy, and to them, they do not understand us, because they seek patterns, because they do not understand that they do not have the gift of spiritual power, and they are easily predicted by the intelligence of Immortalaeism. To not be understood by their cultures is a sign that he is not a part of their empire, and that he sees the cosmic, instead of today's worlds order. In order to learn more about his culture, he must fully accept his self-governance, and he will see that the possibility of his training will bring the full world into view, and that all as changed in his eyes, and the illusions of things, so that he may view things clearly, and understand his privilege as a hero.

He must not see the world any longer, but he must see through the world, and see the spirit. The world is a labyrinth of false signals, but how should he see through them if he cannot understand how to look? There is no path, no one that understands the way, he must accept that there is a higher way to use the world, and that there is a higher way than the world, and he will be beyond civilization. The civilization that is apparent in the world is only a reflection of what people have understood in the stages of their lives, it is life and death, it is the end. Immortalae must not use civilization blindly, it is only a representation of what they have thought is needful for the spirit, and the Immortalae must be guided by greater spiritual belief. It is not necessarily what is needful. What is needful is that all of his needs are met, so that he can understand how to progress in life. So what is culture, but a distraction, an illusion, and a lie. It is a lie, because it is not actually meant for him, it prevents him from understanding his truth. It feeds his appetite, but it does not provide the assurance of furtherance in the spectrum of self-governance. He will never understand how to be himself, if he never acknowledges himself, but to do so, he must leave all influences, he must allow the meditations of life to take him into the reality of his true consciousness, without witness, free and without abuse. He must see the way forward, to progress, and to the things that he needs, and he will not know the way, until he understands the truth of who he is. There are many ways by which one must understand himself, but this is only a beginning and it is the way to being able to understand how to comprehend himself without error, and he will understand then the true problems of his inner self, he will possibly see that he has no character flaw, and then he is ready to begin, and to wage is conflict in the world, to understand how to begin because he understands his own life. The power of moving problems out of the way by understanding the proper dominions of personality is freedom to the soul, and healing and restoration from the world. It matters that in the freedom, he understands how to relate to the world, because he does not need their influence, and he does not believe in their lies. In the lie, there is no truth in life, and he is without acceptance from the intention of his divine ascendancy. He will not understand it if he does not leave the world, and its influence. The safety of self-preservation from others will mean that he must probably accomplish this in secrecy, unless he has a true mentor. A true mentor will provoke the path to him, but he will not lead him, he must choose on his own that he understands the way of self-empowerment, and to allow his being to find its own way out of the darkness, the abuse and illusion. His reluctance to follow anything at all in the world, and instead to retreat to isolation and meditation is a sign that he does not want what the world has to offer, and he desires to understand his life from within himself, and to understand his own spirit. He will never be the man he is supposed to be if he does not understand that he is lost and following with the lost. This is the process of self-realization, and in self-realization, he must allow himself to graduate to an understanding that is beyond the lust and temptation of society, and also beyond its dictates of his time and meaning in the world. He must also not listen to many voices, he must hear the sound that calls him to greater realization, and this is his spiritual path that will guide him in understanding what the world is. Before he left the world, he understood what the definitions of things meant, but now that he understands that he is beyond civilization, he understands the full integration of himself, in regard to the qualities that govern in society, and he finds his place. He must understand what those qualities are to him, but without societal influence. The use of a society that has understood in-front of him is only useful in as far as that society has understood it, if he uses societies regulation instead of his own thought. He will hear, but he must not listen to every voice, once he finds himself in power. He will understand before they speak, and in a higher state, it is easy to predict their governances. He will hear that which is for him in the world, and he will see it, and he will not know every voice, and he will not entertain every lustful image. He cannot arrive there without discipline, and without realization. He may think that he needs to understand the martial art, because he thinks that is his interest, but that is not the objective. The objective is that he realizes himself as a martial artist as a strong male, and then he will understand that he understands martial arts and the spirit of it, and not the formal understanding to its definition and guidance. He must realize himself, and then he will understand what to do. The world is predictable in this manner, and the patterns that arise in its modus. It is the same as saying that he becomes aware and a part of a higher intelligence than is in the world, because by being non-participant, he understands that the use of something, is the rejection of another, and thus, it is a matter of how one uses the construct that reflects what is his spirituality, but also, that he will see that he can predict the manner of the world that is not self-realized, and they do not understand him. When he begins to hear differently, and to see through icons, images, lusts, and representations, he is communicating with higher intelligence, and he must remain at this time, that it is his every thought and impulse that guide his progress, and he must develop his behaviors into traits and character, so that he may reside in a high spiritual state. If it is martial arts, then he will be very deeply moved into forms and techniques, and he will cut through bronze with the depth of his meditative movements. When he becomes aware of the thoughts of his impulse and spirit, and he becomes aware of higher power, he will understand that some things must be the way that they are, because of the governance of power that is guiding it, and he will understand the balance and harmony of things in respect to power. He will understand that the intelligence of the spirit is always correct, in accordance with what it performed in experience. He will understand that in order to meditate, he must quiet his spirit, and in the spirit his internal energy, he must push away his false desires, and he must accept a new shore, and attempt to maintain that accomplishment in the spirit by letting it permeate the consciousness, and become habitual. Power does not make a mistake, so he is responsible that his desires were his selections, and they granted him a deserved spirituality. Culture does not understand the possibility of self-realization, and some things in the spirit will not be expressed into the tangible, physical world. Culture does not understand self-realization because it does not understand how to explain that he can understand without thinking, and he can ascend by ascetic impulsivity and graduate by silence because it is the messages of culture and popularism that have brought his mind into distraction. Culture is the expressive and the pride, it is the loud and in modern culture, they lust for its images, and the lust that in the future, they will not understand their lives, but that they will be seen in a certain respect, as is admired in culture. The hero does not believe in popularism, he does not believe in fame or celebrity, he does not believe in lust, but that he understands something, because he knows it in experience. He understands that power has perfect implementation, and that this is a behavior that he may use to posture himself. The navigation of the being, the rudder, is the mouth. To pronounce is always the way of direction, to speak in one's domain, is to command. The pronunciation of the spirit brings its future into reality, and the impulse of thought dictate the state. As to reject a book is to reject its ideas. The truth in the cosmos understands that there is higher meaning, and the entire construct is marvelous, as truth communicates its manifold understanding, the implications from higher meaning are dynamic, as he looks into the construct of the cosmetic world. This universal intelligence speaks in high regard, it is the connection of the cosmos to man and his construct. As nature does not build houses, so mans construct is unique, and he attempts to make it personal, social, worldly, and universal. The expression of dominion in written maxims are always statements that refer to dominion, as they express the governance of a rule. In order to reach higher dominion, his thoughts must comply with its rule, so that he is accepted. The being must withdraw in meditation and abstain from worldly and cultural forms. Ascendancy in this manner is the necessity of heroes, because they need to understand themselves without society, and they must be intelligent. In order to lead he must understand the dominion of power, in earthly realms and also astral power and governance, and he must understand that culture is a distraction, and the many spirits of the world, and how one may select them in different arrangements, is something that the hero must escape, he must reject culture, in order to realize himself and fill himself with his true life and path.

His path must cross with that of the hero. He will see through the domain of civilization, and he will understand that his life becomes lit with the candle of true spirituality when he no longer needs the world. He will be above vice, and his character will not tempt something such as covetousness. He will understand the world because when he sees what he understands, and he understands it because he does not use the world to see it with him. He is a god in the world now, a god of war, because he is seeing things in immortal ways because it is timeless to see it all at once. He will now understand that there are greater things for him, because there is more in the spirit. Any pattern he does not understand, is foreign or a higher dominion. He will understand the patterns if he understands that there is no one again. He will understand it because his truth will see through it, as long he does not violate his truth. All people have different truths, including evil men. A personal truth is a governance that understands his relation. His full governance and relation are his preferences and character. Which is the hero. He will see the entirety of the spirit and its edifices and spiritualities, and he will go over the city in order to place the city below himself in the spirit and he will see the end of the city in the height of the spirit, and he will understand the spirituality, and he will understand what happens, so that he is properly directed according to the spiritual edifice. The world, its systems and terminals are influenced by the demonic, he must tear off the chains that pull him and break the chains of the establishment despite their outward claim, regain spiritual inner peace, and he must see the end of the city, because that is the end of his life, it is the world's illusion that is before him physically, but underneath is the spiritual terminals (ends) of the world, it is the problem that defines the complexity of the society, and what the people have becomes spiritually. (The opportunity to fight against the demonic, for the hero, is in the city. This is available for the Immortalae, because of demons and powers that aggress in the spirit, and in the flesh.) The patterns and circumstances must be recognized and 'over-stepped' in order to arrive at the destination, that is, at the full truth of the circumstance. He must demand the real circumstance in order to be involved in what is taking place. He must meet the requirements of the fight. He will face lesser realities if he does not know it, he will encounter a similar circumstance, to a lesser degree.

There is no civilization except the cosmos and victory.
His real rank and office are in the authenticity of his spirit universally.

He finds his way through the world by looking at death's
mark.
He finds a higher Power by looking through civilization.
He comes to a personal truth.

Arcade

Training (Universal)

The arcade is the battle formation, all of the setting and variable and parameters. To take a hill. To siege castle walls. To fight in winter. To fight against the demonic. To be placed in modern warfare in a city. To be in a martial arts fight, fighting with hands and fists. To rescue the woman. To save the townsfolk from a burning church. To Unite as Double-Dragon. To fight in the streets against crime. To save an important blood-line. To recover strategic information. To fight for the end of mankind. To Assault. To charge a battlefield. To shoot down aircraft. To fight with the blessings of wolves. To battle Artificial Intelligence. To fight in guerilla warfare. To fight a conspiracy. To unbind curses. The Magick of the Earth.

The arcade is the edifice that one fights in. It conveys the strategy and the points of contact, the storyline and all of the details. The spiritualism Immortalaeism has an arcade from which it specializes in fights and training. Concept-gaming is all arcades for circumstances that could transpire in the real world. The Immortalae must specialize in training in the arcade, and this is a part of our religion of heroism. Immortalaeism supports whatever training is necessary and concept-games are a starting point for the Immortalae to realize his possibilities, and his mastery.

The Immortalae must begin with the dragon, and he must be a hero. He will be in the saga and the interplay of fighting in the cosmos. He will be a Guardian of Civilization. He is masterless, and will not be ruled. He will understand power and Immortality and fighting. This is where all Immortalae must begin. Once they understand this, then they have the arcade.

Dragon

Symbol of Immortalaeism

In my teaching, I call them, both male and female, to train as an immortal warrior. I do not condemn that women are not capable of achieving the full merit of my teachings and authority. In pairs, if needed, or alone, they will accept the understanding of Immortalaeism, immortality, heroism and martial arts, and they will venture as a firm into the problems of life, and they will understand what it is to be above and in control of what is happening, because they understand that they are above them because they do not understand the circumstance because they think that they are not intelligent. The intelligence of power (Power I, II, III) is for the development of virtue, and the personal energy of power (Coac) and one's dominion, and to understand what I have said about culture and the Immortalae identity (Heroism and Dragon) is the beginning of the teaching, in practicum. The group must be fully devoted to the cause of Immortalaeism and immortality, which are the induction into teaching, and they will, in the end, be fully developed and they will understand that leadership belongs to no one, and that they are not ruled, and that they should understand that as a group, united, they can overcome any feat or problem, and that they will accomplish a reach into the cosmic powers that rule and govern the Earth and Heavens, and they will accept the Dragon in order to accept Immortalae. In the world, they will have difficulty, difficulties that have been known for ages, of patterns of deviousness and depravity that come in the world, that target what is valuable. I understand what many of these problems are, that are generated by ageless evils. The dragon is the greater spirit to master these issues of the conflict between virtue and vice, and its power that carries them, a spirit that will not fail, it is a spirit that is eternal, and does not die, and it is a spirit that will call them, individually, and expect that they meet the full maturity of their lives and calling. The dragon has overcome the power of wickedness and evil, and thus, he has overcome the fires of damnation, so he takes them in his nostrils, he understands the eternal, and rests in a high spiritual place, and he sleeps and guards the fortunes of treasure, and he can see through both good and evil, and he is not burned by the poison of the snake. The dragon will take a warrior with it and he will carry them over time and position and teach him to think martial arts and war in regard to the ageless teachings. The dragon will situate them in a fight. It understands harmony of times and divines how a warrior should be inserted into an altercation. The dragon sees the opening of the Immortalae-eternal in the midst of the mortal world, and translates epochs and times, and because it is eternal, it sees the opportunity of the Immortalae in the world, his place of destiny and combat.

The sign of the Eternal and Immortal, the symbol of Immortalaeism, is a dragon. I have chosen the dragon also because the snake is cursed with being the lowest of all creatures, but the dragon has overcome its predicament but it is not an innocent creature, but has known hellish things. Snakes are venomous and poisonous, a weapon from immunity. Snakes are a representation of Immortalaeism's Sovereignty, a fire which the snake cannot escape from, as if caught on fire by Sovereignty. A snake that is depicted eating its own tail is a symbol of continuous life, opposed to being cursed, its ability to shed its skin and to go through so many life cycles, is a symbol of Processionalism, that while it begins where it ends, and ends where it began, a graduation occurs which brings it into a new life, life Eternal. The dragon is a snake that has the ability to consume fire, and the ability to fly, relinquishing its hellish curse to slither as the lowliest of creatures. Having escaped its original curse, it flies, and having overcome the fires of destruction, it may now consume it with its mouth, and breathe fire. Having overcome death, and knowing both good and evil, it is now a symbol of the Immortals and of Immortality in the spirituality that is 'Immortalaeism' as a symbol of powerful goodness. It means that we were once the deadliest men in the fall of mankind, but we have found immortality, we are now dragons, having overcome both good and evil (introduction, Immortalaeism III).

The Dragon can see him through the most wicked of evils, and it will take him through life, through the monotony of society, because it is not convinced by and subtleties of men, or gods, and it will supply his spirit with the spirit of fighting. It can find other men that are dragons, as all of the Immortalae are dragons. In the days to come there will be great conflicts and difficulties, because they are the burden of this world. The Dragon will consume himself in martial arts, and he will be esoteric in the knowledge of fighting. The Dragon is what he is to resemble. He must understand conversions, architecture and design, he must understands 'sets' that are equal in power and expertise. The Dragon will unite with his spirit in the spirit of Immortalaeism (which is the spirit of fighting, of power, of immortality and heroism). They will find one another because they know the Dragon, and they will find each other because they do not know anything else.

Double-Dragon

The dragons are over and above in spirituality in the eternal dimension, they are calling the eternal, steeped in the understandings of immortality and the martial way, and they are choosing a special people. Two dragons over two lives holding a common plot (conjuring) and fate, means that the induction of two will be drawn together in life, and their destinies are united, at least for a time. They share a common fate, and they understand that they are respectfully bound to the same purpose, as equals.

Double Dragon is a word I use for two of either the Eternals or the Immortals which means that the two individuals will become twins (Gemini), and they will share one fate. Hitting one hits the other, and a success for one is a success for the other, a champion and a champion, fighting together. Their eternal and immortal energies are combined in the everlasting, a perfect harmony. The two lives are intertwined in the fabrics of destiny, and they have the same destiny as well for as long as they are together. The dragons of Immortalaeism are not tempted, and they will understand the complications of guile, and they will bear no prejudice. The double dragon will not understand how that one would desire something of someone else, in temptation. He is available for eternal and immortal ways, and in the end, he is the one that understands eternal life or immortality, and he has a fight in the world, and he has the beginning of what will last forever in his life. He will accept that he is a person that is capable of great dynamic lifestyle, and he will be free in the world – he will cultivate true character, and he will not be persuaded by the cultures or opinions of the world. The symbol of double dragon is two snakes intertwined in a symbol, eating one another's tail, beyond death, where both beginning and end of both are interwoven as one.

Double Dragon demonstrates exemplary virtue, and instead of learning through life alone, they may learn from one another, knowing that their consciousness is united, bound to one other with an Immortal bond. Double Dragon is a bond that is formed past death. It is an eternal or an immortal relationship that spans time as an unbreakable connection, a oneness that is beyond death, a device of Eternal and Immortal society.

The dragons are forming a nexus throughout time, calling two or more destined warriors into their plan, through time. The dragons reflect the identity of the warrior they select, because they understand how to divine the circumstance as a dragon, because they collect the same circumstance from the world. Weaving an eternal knot and bond, the dragons develop their own microcosmic selection of talented/perfect warriors, a collection and a small representation for the ages. The dragon, over the ageless evils and times, understands the maturity of the fight, and that the Immortalae may also understand the full wisdom of such fights, he is capable of guiding the spirit of the Immortalae into the society of Immortality and the martial way. The dragon is the symbol of our Eternal and Immortal emblem, the culture of Immortalaeism.

NOT ALL ARE CHOSEN.
IMMORTALAEISM.

DRAGON

...he does not understand anymore, he will not awaken, he has been consumed...the dragon has him.
                    - Vaul Impera

Darkness

The dragon waits, drenched in darkness beyond the limits of your reasonable and non-combatant, civilized mind. He thinks they will never understand him, because their minds are filled with the success of society. He waits for you to understand in darkness, rather than the traces and the lines of civility. As in the dark ages, we grow accustomed to seeing in the dark. He is gripped and driven by compelling forces away from the shackles of civilized life. On the border of the civilized mind he waits. In the deliberation of the man's civilized soul he surrenders his wit against society, he will not be a part of it. He can hear the over-emotion in their expression, he can see the signs of poor mental understanding in their demonstrations. They cannot hear, and they cannot see. Won't you leave, before the foolish face of society consumes you with its teeth, making you a part of their charade, in the light? So he leaves.

The darkness has gripped you and driven you and drawn you, and now you do not see anymore that in society you have a life that is worth living. The unmanifested spirit has brought you, and we know that it is unmanifested, don't we? He could have spent another fifteen years in the avarice and vanity and mental gluttony of the machine that drives society. His mind and your confession would conform, and his spirit would be broken to its device. All this is in the light! Wayward signs, filthy projects, crooked authorities, and a prize for you, if you can beat the system. Most of all, a will that has been punched by concession, that does not know how to believe in anything else. So you have left. But how do we fully leave?

I cannot hear their call. I do not see anything desirable. But how do I know that I have left society? I do not understand their plans or organizations, their mediums or their business. It is futility, absurdity. I do not understand the pretense of their emotion, or the direction of their lives. I cannot pretend that I understand their point of view. I hear a pure society, the society that I understand that I am from; I see blasphemy before me, in the form of business, and I need to begin to live a life that I will not regret, and it is not a part of this social madness.

He is gripped by darkness, and drawn into it, he feels freedom in escape, in loneliness without witness. He sees darkness all around him and his contrite spirit begins communicate over the city, in the absence of its distraction. He only needs it in order to know that he is not of its edifice, because the indication that he is leaving and that something is calling him is indicated by what transpires in society. It is not that the city is not there, it is that his life is being translated and traversing into another spiritual place. The profundity that the city is meaninglessness. It is not the darkness of the rampant corruption of the society that is unintelligent to him or darkness in itself, darkness is isolation, realizing that he is not a part of society. In this is freedom. He seeks to fill himself and his life with this darkness, to gird himself from distraction that bothers his meditation about what society is to him, the realization of his suspicions, he desires to move forward into darkness.

The dragon is waiting, clothed in darkness. As the dragon is in darkness, so must he be. The dragon is steeped in non-civilization, it calls to him as tortured, it waits at the gates where he finally leaves society. He has starved for the truth of society, he pained to see its true face, and its end, he races to progress in society to no real avail. He wants to get rid of its residue, and filth and impression, so he covets the darkness, to clothe himself in it, to hide himself from their disease. He desires to lose his mind of civility, and social patterning. He will leave and never return.

In the darkness, is everything that he has been looking for. Escape, performing without society, independence, truth, isolation, freewill, destiny, freedom from societies restraint. Now he can truly know himself, and now can he truly know fighting. The darkness has brought him to his liberation, he must seek the darkness to find why it has delivered him. He has been released to know another life, and he has been freed so that he may be able to be a fighter.

He must recognize the intelligence of this move, in which he did not desire society, but that he was released from it, and it was holding him from martial arts and fighting. The dragon must have been fair, in order to offer him a fair fight, without the restraint of society. He has been resisting society his entire life, and he does not wish to pursue its aims, in this I deduce that his enemy is within society, or that he was using its measure because it brings him into bondage. Before long, he would have been locked in society, unable to resist his opponent, delivered to his whims.

The limitation and the imputation of society presumes that he will be found repeatedly in the same composure. His immobility means prediction, it means that he can be intersected and attacked. It is all of the lines of society and its reason that brings him through the streets on time each day. The resources and the elements of society determine that what is necessary for him must be obtained by participation and conformity. The dragon will watch as countless numbers are frozen in commerce and responsibility because they cannot escape the jaws of society's grasp, they can never quite free themselves ultimately. They have moments of clarity in which they do not see themselves on the grid of society, but never fully the wisdom of its warning, they become enticed by its grasp before long, and it consumes their mind. The witness of society hides many in the lusts of their spirits, they are unapproved below the surface of civility and professional life. They need society so that they may use its discipline to conform their spirits from blasphemy. Those who leave society must use the resources of society, but they do not use society in order to obtain their requirements. The dragon waits in deep darkness, and it has no semblance of society in its understanding, it does not understand why they think with society. The dragon, in darkness, will never be understood by someone who thinks with society. When he reaches it, they will never understand him, but he will understand them. He will understand that they are caught in the grasp of society, and that they cannot begin to understand the way of martial arts, street fighting, or any other occupation that means that he does not belong with society's civility. Those who are in society never understand who they are, because they do not believe in themselves without its inspiration. When they reach the dragon, they find why they understand things. The way of fighting is to make the way in the world's opportunities by applying the talent of combat, and for some, there is no other way than street fighting in order to be anything in the world. His ways are covered in darkness, because his opportunity is without the approval of society. The darkness consumes him, and he views that many view that most things in life are a means to an end, and that it is this deafness and blindness that he cannot understand, as though he hears a truth speaking to him of vanity. Society is searching for the image of a greater self, and it is his despair to view that he must understand always what is in the spirit of society's ego. He hears the demonic. He desires that his place is without society, and that he should be spared to leave its bearing on him, so that he may become what he sees without society, because he see's the way of honor and martial arts, and he see's that the temporary claims of society will not entice him, not for society's prize. There is no prize, because they do not understand him, and because they do not understand his reason, he must be prepared to fight. He has many fights, and many natural enemies, and he must understand the way of fighting, and how to fight, because he must fight for his life, and he must challenge against opponents with respect and honor. Outside of society, to which none are enticed, is the dragon, who understands all things as they are, as martial combat. The way of fighting is not apparent to them, they are not given the same respect, because they do not understand on their own that they have a place that they can accept and understand before society, because society rejects their notion, so that they cannot find a place except to be given one, and those who have found darkness will not accept the places of society.

They may not challenge all of society, but they will be accepted by those who do not feel that they can make a presentation in society's firm, and be placed in recognition, because they have more intelligence than they do, because they are not provoked by society's leadership.

There can be no peace with the ignorance of society, when doors close by the hundreds, they will not forgive him because they mistake him intentionally and in society, justice wanders away so that he can become nothing out of his promise. I presume that I can manage everything without society, that society must respond to my progress I make on my own, and promotion is close, but I will believe in their respects, and not in fact, and it is this opinion to which I hate – that I know that I should leave, because I cannot blame society for its positions, and I must perform independently, there is nothing before me when society is not apparent. I understand that I cannot accept society's conditioning, so I will condition myself, and I will become a martial artist, and the centre of my conditioning is that I understand myself in full control of my intelligence, and not controlled by society. Society will try to control me, but I owe them no respects.

Society will respect the mentality and the order that it provides for its own. In this schooling is what the dragon will not understand, it understands all of society, but does not agree with its way of life. The dragon will accept that those who it discovers will possess no blemish in their character, a fully capable individual who is not in disagreement with what is required in the cosmos of the world, because he will demonstrate that he is of pure mind, strong and masculine. The darkness has brought him through his enemies' territory, away from its stronghold. The chains that are brought through society's agreement are bonds that lock him into holds and make him vulnerable. His power is subtly sifted and channelled into his enemies' stronghold, it will bring him into submission of will, if possible, breaking his power and his will against his agreements. He no longer has the opportunity of choice.

The power of the darkness becomes his character, and presumes his personality and spirituality. He must understand the world without society, he must not understand society in order to understand the real world. He must understand the spirits, which determine what is within the world of society and the world without society, the composition. He must hear and see properly, which is that he must hear the ambitions and vanities of the intention and the false-life, he must hear what people seek for themselves when they are communicating. He must see that covetous ambition is the resolve, and arrogance that is within society, sometimes due to avarice, and self-gain. The spirituality of the matter lies within the honesty and the regard of those who do not use society as a means to garner an image of a pleasure in false-ego. Many in society must cover their iniquities, and outside of society there is no apparatus which supports lofty self-indulgence of character. Darkness is freedom from this apparatus, to see the spirituality of the world without what men can seek in guile from each-other. The criminal will not pay a false respect or give false authority, but the man of society does. It is in wanting from the populous and deriving a sense of prominence from their approval that is a grand vanity in his imagination. It is here that we begin to accept martial arts, because we do not trust society to manage our discrepancies, because I do not use society except that I must win in society, and thus I will understand justice and equity, but I do not trust the justice of society ultimately, because they understand that they want to become something, and something to people, but the things that they do are only a means to this end. We do not trust society, or the world, so we take martial arts (dark arts). We consume ourselves in darkness, away from society's influence, so that we may gain a clear and uncorrupted mind in the sight of the world. We abase our false knowledge, ridding false pride, arrogance, vanity, self-gain, luxuries so that we may finally see our way through the world. The worlds imagination, how it runs impetuously measuring our scales, theories, reasonings, is an illusion and a witticism that we run from. It possesses us with its will and causes us to run in its fashion, to death, in the pursuits of lusts and vices. These mountains of accomplishment must be moved outside of society and not in vanity, it must rest without the expectation of hubris, in a true estimation of character.

Martial Arts

In self-discipline and in our spirituality, and with the Dragon, we assume martial arts. Martial arts without society is pragmatic and it is our spiritual engagement, that we understand hand-to-hand combat, and that we are intellectually competent and we pursue self-mastery. The dragon will lead to the form that is without form, because he is the abasement of instruction. In the essence of martial combat, which the dragon will lead to, is that we think remembrance, and then the essence is gone. It is that this apparent/non-apparent relationship causes us to focus on the true meaning of our inspiration, and that mentality is systematic response, automatic, whereas in free-form, that ability of movements are perfected into the form of the martial art, but then the instruction must be broken in order to allow ingenuity and true potential. We must allow the dragon to break our form, so that we do not lose the true meaning and essence of our martial art, and that of our spirituality, so that we are broken from society, and then we are built up in self-mastery and the essence of true martial arts. We must reach the fullness of proper fighting, and we must be ready at all times for what transpires in the world. In martial arts, we are not those who protect the interests of others because we are not in the level of fighting where we think that people are under our authority. Martial arts is for those who understand they have a problem in the world and it is their problem because they do not believe that they are understood. In street fighting, he is capable of determining what happens to him from the time he is young, and without this resistance, anything can happen, so that he will not know his own favor, only the disrespect of others and their effects on his behalf. Martial arts is the art of expression in knowing that to fight is to overcome a circumstance. He will know fighting because he understands the way, and the way must begin with virtue.

Without society, he will understand hand-to-hand combat in martial arts, and he will know his dominion in the regard of his ability in intellect and in fighting. In unrestricted potential, the martial artist will become supremely powerful through his ability to fight (to be adverse, to resist). Yet, it is always through the ability to fight that the martial artist understands that he has anything at all, and that his dominion is kept by martial arts, and the concourse that he possesses in self-mastery. He must know his ability over the entire world, or else it is in vain. The dragon rests apart from the world, reaching those who come and thirst for the way without society, the true principles of the world, and not the triviality of men. In darkness it waits to fashion warriors at the height of the world, drawing them from their place in civility, so that they may taste the raw power of martial combat and its effectiveness, and how it empowers the spirit and soul. If there was something inside of the palm of an open hand, martial arts is a closed fist. Martial arts understands fighting and the human nature, so that it will not reveal to anyone what it thinks. In martial arts, people never understand why, because they cannot think him. In martial arts people cannot believe what he says, because they can never believe what he thinks. In martial arts, they never understand what to think, because they are opposed. In martial arts, they never operate in my understanding, because they cannot comprehend my actions. In martial arts, they never understand what I believe [opinion], so I fight with them.

In hand-to-hand combat, he will master the inner energy field, and he will develop harmony with his abilities, and he will unite fighting to all of his ways. Society says civil arrest, the martial artist think aggression. To be in darkness he will separate with society, he must be a martial artist at all times, and not in convenience, he must see the need to fight at any time, that he sees his opponents glaring at him night and day in the societal cage, devouring his time and labor, as if he were a slave. The dragon has come to liberate him, to bring the full potential of his martial art, and to covet that he cannot lineate with the aims of society. He is set-free in darkness and in fighting. In street fighting he has a way of not losing his own respect, and this is the only way for him, because he cannot accept what society has to offer. Ultimately, he may become the champion of society, but he will not understand them, because they will not understand the circumstance of his time in the world, because he fought evils, he upsets the credulity of the people.

The presence of darkness, the presence of time and self and self-realization, and the notion of a prevalent leading force in society that is in discrepancy with his, contribute to the need for martial arts. The self, in society, is produced through the civility and discipline of humility, and as society does, it fixes their position with the lead of the people, and it is in this digression that he finds distaste, because he hates the leadership of their wanton desire, and their practiced civilization and etiquette, which bears no real semblance within his understanding. In this context, he will not understand society any longer, he will not understand its ways, except that he understands that he requires resource and he understands that this is the way of society, that they will not understand who you are, unless they derive what they desire from him through disrespect and degradation. The system of the society that is inhabited is talent driven / utilitarian, and in this manner in society for works, he will win regard. Martial arts is in the regard of the dragon, and opposition by not being a part of society, and in this manner, it will find that he will not understand society, and he will become stronger because he will understand the darkness, and no longer understand the society in which he lives. Society is always seeking allure and prestige, always willing to make a slave, and it is never in the way of martial arts. They will never understand him, and he will not give his credit into society, and hustle the gossip and the opportunity. In this manner, society would have him in its teeth, ready to devour him because he is understanding of society's leadership. Society is apt to sell and trade him, and he is tiresome of this game, he will not accept its mercantilism, he desires that he would be in charge of his economy, so that he is not drawn by temptation or necessity or desire into a shackle. The dragon and martial arts do not approve of such commerce, and will not accept its ways. The martial artist will prove that he is in control by not being enticed in society's business.

In darkness, he will dawn a head covering and a face covering, and he will select a colour of preference in martial arts, and he will mask his face so that he is not easily understood by providing information with his glances, and he will develop muscle as part of his program in order to face an opponent in fighting, he must train in martial arts. The dragon understands that aside from convention, that it is dangerous to be revealing, that it is his own protection from the imbibing of society that he must prevent, because society makes imparting invitation if he selects attire that is meant to show society that he is interested in provoking them, and in this respect, he must be modest and well clothed. The dragon will accept his darkness, and in this manner of dress, he has satisfaction, as a basis for attire. The dragon must understand what it means in order to leave society, it must understand his problem, beyond a lifetime of civility. The civility will perish with lust, but the dragon must visualize that the dragon-warrior is beyond time, that his venture and his purposes will make sense when he is no longer alive. He must not provide many projections so that he cannot be anticipated, and he must not always give his opinions so that he cannot be duplicated. He must be as prudent as a dragon. He must not leave any traces, except for those things for which he has come. He must be mannerly, masculine and clean and intelligent and shrewd in order for this to occur. He will not provoke a fight, he will be silent and over-looking (high) of his surroundings, so that he will be correctly judged in the first place in regard to fighting. He will be professional and he will understand the demonic if he needs to, and he will be understanding of religious concepts especially due to immortality and pre-determination. He is drawn and guided by the dragon, who always manifests an answer to his intelligence, and leads to the unmanifested, where in the unmanifested is the realm of his spiritual inquiry, where he can understand what is behind the world, *for him*. From his angle of spiritual investigation, he understands the nature of the world, and he attempts to understand the metaphysical in order to understand the influence of the unmanifested on reality.

In martial arts, he must break the form of the system of martial combat, and he is similar in this to breaking the form of society, because its instruction and rigidity have given him a practiced and as uniform response to all that is around him. He pains in order to arrive at the dragon and the darkness, because he needs to understand why society has a problem that encourages him to delve deep into consciousness to find a way away from the worlds subconscious views that keep him as a false capita in its regency and spends all of his time in destitution. He must quicken in martial arts once he is in darkness. So much time is given into problems in the world, and this is the rate at which his enemy could be moving. He must be vigil, and he must be accurate; he will understand his enemy when he no longer lives, either because he wants something, or in persecution though he has not done anything at all.

The world is ever spinning, and there are many wants and desires, many aggressions, many agreements that must be enforced, but the dragon will not understand them, because it does not understand who they could be, 'because they do not understand *who I am* (who the dragon is)'.

Dragon

Truth the dragon says, is in circumstance generally, but my truths are in martial arts, self-mastery and meditation. Though there are many truths, and governing realisms that provide for such things as reasonability, it is circumstance that he must understand, and he must believe that he will be the one, the dragon-warrior, because he only see's the dragons fight in martial arts in the world. There is no one in the world that can understand the dragon because he does not reveal himself to them. They will not understand him because he will not show them what it means because they are not his. The spirit of the dragon is in darkness and it will not see any light except the unmanifested manifesting in circumstance. In deep darkness, it sees the horror of the machine of society, of despair and vanity and its deep destruction in the spirits of men. The depiction that is in truth, of the image of society is in the quality and the death of man. The dragon will not understand men who do not behave appropriately and they do not understand their circumstances. The dragon is not in the right mind at any time, because he does not believe in those that wish to understand him. He will believe in a sombre young man because that is truth to his will, and he will believe in a protector as a man, because that is the truth of society. The dragon will not understand who a person is if they do not understand how a man makes something of himself in the world. The man who the dragon selects will not be given to covetousness, he will not understand wealth except in true value, and will not seek wealth. He will not be improper or of incorrect estimation. He will challenge the status quo. The dragon will see his fight in the world because of what is against him because of who he is.

The dragon will watch as many men bite on what is available at the table of life, but only those who do not accept from the hands of society will find satisfaction in the darkness of the spirit, and to whom the dragon may reveal itself. The dragon draws with spirituality, it draws by understanding that the city of corrupt man was built against his pre-determination, and that he would not understand how to accommodate what it thinks of successfulness. The dragon finds a man that is undivided in his thought that he must learn without the influence of society, that he is pure from the corruption of societal thought, and he has reserved his life for one teaching and martial art. This undefiled consciousness will find other dragon-warriors that do not understand what they could want in society, or achieve in its own view. The view of society is an unrealistic imagination, a picture of domestic life that is without martial arts, that lacks true male leadership, it does not understand fighting, and it is partitioned in agreements that bend him and break him in various ways so that he cannot perform the full duties of masculinity. Many desire to host, and to be great communicators and negotiators that are in society, men of business and renown for exploit and excellence, and it is in this aggrandizement of business that the dragon-warrior must understand that his primary focus is disciplines and martial arts, and that they who perform such an office are applauded in society for their work, but the work of the dragon is martial arts. The dragon-warrior is given to law, because the digression of conflict is what he must understand, and he understands military because in war he has his own place. He also understands the priesthood, because he understands how to negotiate his own spirit in excellence in order to fashion what is in his spirit, which is martial arts. In this, he is not losing time in his disciplines in the world. He will become more useful. The dragon spirit will require his direct and sole attention, for him to clear his mind of outside influences and to acquire the true meaning of martial arts and to understand that society has a place for him in the end, and that it is exposed to mischief and all blasphemy that could contrive against his time and end, and to expose only that he had labour, no matter the occupation, but that his office in society was fictitious, and that his worth was not counted. The devil is truly annoying in this stage, a jest that the vanity of society brings disapproval in the end, and anonymity of regard and reputation, after years of contribution. They do not remember their own well, it is usually the just and the truly noble that provide dignity, and great talent forces compulsion. The dragon-warrior must understand that the relationships of society are not meaningful because they are always a representation of a division of power that is stored in credits, but the dragon-warrior does not allow society to credit him, because he must convey his true meaning. They do not say anything for him. He will not stand to see society's face at the end of a lifetime of labour, he detests their charade.

The dragon perceives that your intelligence will master the feats of the world, he will conceal when you have left for darkness that there is only fighting in the world, nothing else, because it is him against the world, for his entire life, and nothing else, unless he finds true understandings and relationships in people that are strong in martial arts. All else is an illusion. He will conceal to you that there is no opportunity in the world if you are a part of society, and no purpose, and that it is the inability to break the system of the city that is the second aspect, beyond that society is an enemy. All fight for appointment, because the seats are ambiguous and cannot be taken without criticism or approval. What is at the height of society, or at the base? There is no other time but now, and no other place but here. The dragon-warrior will not think that he is not in his proper place because he understands that he is always in his proper place because where he is, is where the honesty of his self has brought him in the realization of his self-mastery, which is the only place that he could be. The agreements of society anger his temper because they restrict his martial art, but desire him as a slave. It is slavery that is disguised by a bank account, but evident in mind and character. He will conceal to you that you owe society nothing, and society says that it owes you nothing, and that you have nothing in its view. You must realize that that is all society will ever be to you, and that you have nothing with society because you do not understand that they choose not to understand you. The society that is given is not a society that will be the one to be something of fulfillment because it does not understand true spirituality. They will not understand you in the end, because they do not understand unless they have something to gain from you.

The dragon will call when the world in its illusion and mask begins to come off. We desire to understand fundamentally in order to get ourselves proper, but we cannot escape the layers of illusion in the world, and how do we get out? Wrapped in understandings that are false, the dragon is the constant that guides the way out. The dragon sees the unmanifested because it anticipates all of their action in a pre-determined manner. In order to understand the unmanifested, you must lose society, because they never see it coming. They make the same gestures, and they never see it coming because they are involved in its scheme. The unmanifested is the point of occurrence that brings in the here and now, a point of creation. In recognizing the present moment, he is actualizing un-attachment to society by not mentally corresponding with its perspective. At this point, he sees the world without influence upon his view. He desires not to be misguided by the world, and he understands that they are not aware of their own behaviour, and he needs to doubt their society, and he needs to be aware of their pretense, so he does not understand them because he cannot fathom their words and their actions and emotions and their reality is without real connotation to him, and he cannot understand how they could possibly determine that they would lead and guide their intelligence in such ways. They have been convinced by a false spirit in society that they need to listen and view and behave in such animations. This spirit is always enticing the mind, getting him to listen, causing him to lose his attention. The spirit wants his time and entertainment, it catches his attention but no matter where it speaks from, it is always the same effect in the end, that he would be without real understanding, caught in the illusion of society and unsophisticated because he does not think without its frame of mind. It wants him to try and see what kind of play he has in society's game, where he believes his possible future and his understanding is involved in it, and this is provided by society's investments. Like a thief in the night it comes to arrest his intelligence, from anywhere in order to seek his inclusion in society. Whatever happens, it is his role and his place in society, as a fixation of the mind, that determines how he is in his temperament and intelligence at that time. He does not see his life in that he is acting this way, but it bears no real understanding except that his ego and his pride have been engaged in playing a game with his life. His successfulness and what it provides to him determine his spiritual state, and in this success the signals he provides in society warrant to him a response from society, and he desires to feel powerful and to make costly actions his entire life, and he desires many things such as family and respect, and he seeks these things his entire life, and because he does not understand the dragon, he does not realize his circumstance. The dragon does not care for any of these things, and it believes that they are weak in their minds, and that they are controlled and they do not understand how to become strong people because of what they have believed about themselves, and there are circumstances and signs that follow that bear evidence to this. The dragon understands that they have lost their minds in society by choice, and that they have desired a method and a way of winning many things to themselves. The dragon will not take such men, any of them, and not those that win the prizes in society. The dragon is looking for the self-confident man that does not accept society, and does not accept that he needs a place with them, because he does not understand them at all. He does not accept them if they do not know anything on their own. He does not believe in them, because they have no real understanding or demonstration in life. He detests their music, their theatre, their games and religion and intellectualism, because they have a false expression of little importance. The dragon will not understand them, because they do not understand life without the false notions of society. The dragon will understand the one that will not take part in their concourse, and will not entertain their aims and prizes. The focus of the dragon-warrior is meditation and to understand himself as a god in the cosmos, by spiritual development he desires immortality and that his countenance cannot tell anymore his understanding, because they cannot think what he thinks. The dragon-warrior will not understand anything anymore, by martial arts and meditation and intellectualism, he will not understand self-aggrandizement in society, and he will be of perfect humility and virtue. His aim is to perfect virtue in order to perfect his character and his works. The dragon-warrior will be exalted over the faults and hypocrisies of men, and he will find expression through martial arts, and he will seek the dragon, who has finished society and the rightful place of the dragon-warrior. He will not entertain society at all, society is for those that are convinced by society. The dragon will encourage his strength and intelligence so that he understands the martial way. The dragon spirit understands the ends of contest by understanding the opponent; it understands the problem of society, but this is only how a life of martial arts *may* begin, in order to think about the world differently. It understands its way of life, and it does not comprehend living as a man of faults and errancy. The dragon spirit enjoys the arcade, it enjoys its strong disciples that are men and women, it enjoys martial training as intelligible men, it enjoys its own perception of the world, it enjoys fighting, it enjoys heroism, it enjoys power, it enjoys immortality, it enjoys weapons training, it enjoying learning and understanding cosmic truth. Most of all, it enjoys fighting with a with a spirit of true understanding of the martial way of life and the mystery of martial arts and the Dragon. In meditation, he practices emptiness.

Civilization

The dragon-warrior must come, and he must come without error. There are many criticisms in the world, but I will provide a list of some of which cannot be found in the dragon-warrior: idiocy, uncertainty, stupidity, cowardice, faultiness, immorality, unsophistication, reprobation, illogical, tempting, divisive, sedition, swelling words of vanity, imbecile, fanatic, zealot, tainted, corrupt, hypocrisy, vice, blasphemy, concupiscence, fear-mongerer. In consequence a dragon-warrior must be predestined/fate, spiritual, powerful, intelligent, mature, masculine/feminine, cultured by 'Immortalaeism', clean, virtuous, excellence, martial arts, strength, power, truth, purity, tasteful.

The dragon-warrior understands that there is no truth in civilization in regard to the said schemes, and he must forge his own path, without its' influence. He must take the guiding spirit, the dragon, and not civilization any longer. He must accept martial arts, and he must accept meditation, and he must not be a part of society. In civilization, he fights against bonds and restraints, and he fights against their way of life, knowing that their prejudice is demonic, and that even the mediocre would desire his demise demonically, in favor of their own ambitions. His civility is demonic, but civilization does not always have to be demonic, it is a symptom of the people's spirituality. It is demonic to always want things from people to which they do not confer or accept, because the vice of their decision converts their confession and their minds to the demonic, and because they do not understand their vanity, they will not believe that there was something that was correct in its decree that their behaviour was wrong. In the animus of the spirit is the method by which their being is converted to the demonic, and why they do not understand that their entire appearance has changed, though of course, they are under the belief that what they have become is intelligent. They make men liable and bring them in under the disguise of civility, in bonds and agreements. The true method of understanding the balance of power and why it is found that the immortal should be superior is difficult to find, but I have made it apparent in this book, Immortalaeism. He understands their civility, but he has left civilization, and he even understands their demonic, but it does not matter, he chooses not to be one of them at all. Civilization holds the academic, and it holds law and justice, but he must understand the dragon, though he has lived in and understood civilization, it no longer holds any promise for him in what he needs to understand about his life and the cosmos. He has sought his true life by leaving civilization, so that he would not be ruled by anything. They think everything to 'the dragon-warrior' when they meet him, because they are slaves to their masters.

He found that civilization was death to him, because he was immobile in it, he was not able to do anything against its persuasion over his cause, and without knowing that he was 'dead' in it, he could not have prevented an untimely death, for a reason that understands little about why he should live in a greater measure and freedom. He understands that it is possible that someone is in charge of this measure taken, but who could it be? It seems it is a false aristocrat that covets the power of prominent people that do not understand they are being taken advantage of. Society has become a trap. But not only a trap, it has become spiritual and intellectual blindness. He cannot understand why civilization has failed to provide him with what he needs, so he must leave. Civilization, the great exploit of communication, has failed our warriors and exploits their privilege and cause, and it does not bring them to know what they must understand about spirituality and the forces of the earth and cosmos. They must break free. He cannot belong when he would be diminished, he has taken his leave, before they attempt to make him stay, and he cannot be more relieved that it is the dragon that will save him and guide him. The dragon is greater than society, and civilization cannot beat the dragon, he will take darkness as a cloak, and he will learn true spirituality, he will learn the dragon. He will evade society, because it no longer matters, and he will find the spirit of his life, and what it says he will consider in his wisdom, and he will understand Immortalaeism and the world, and he will recover his life's purpose. He will become now the hero, and he will understand the dragon. His life may be in danger, because he was going to die without his true purpose, but he was going to die, and even now he is in danger.

He is beginning to understand without the illusion.

THE GATES ARE OPEN
NOT ALL ARE CHOSEN
IMMORTALAEISM